Cover images (left to right): Diana Bishop's parents, Priscilla and Arthur Bishop, Muskoka, 1945/6; Billy Bishop, official RAF photo, 1917; Diana and her brother, Bill, 1958.
Printer: Webcom

Library and Archives Canada Cataloguing in Publication

Bishop, Diana, author
       Living up to a legend : my adventures with
Billy Bishop's ghost / Diana Bishop.

Issued in print and electronic formats.
ISBN 978-1-4597-3770-9 (paperback).--ISBN 978-1-4597-3771-6 (pdf).--ISBN 978-1-4597-3772-3 (epub)

1. Bishop, Diana. 2. Bishop, William A., 1894-1956--
Influence. 3. Television journalists--Canada--Biography.
4. Granddaughters--Canada--Biography. 5. Fighter pilots--
Canada--Biography. I. Title.

PN4913.B54A3 2017   070.4'3092   C2016-906551-0
                                               C2016-906552-9

1   2   3   4   5   21   20   19   18   17

We acknowledge the support of the Canada Council for the Arts and the Ontario Arts Council for our publishing program. We also acknowledge the financial support of the Government of Ontario, through the Ontario Book Publishing Tax Credit and the Ontario Media Development Corporation, and the Government of Canada.

Care has been taken to trace the ownership of copyright material used in this book. The author and the publisher welcome any information enabling them to rectify any references or credits in subsequent editions.
                                               — J. Kirk Howard, President

The publisher is not responsible for websites or their content unless they are owned by the publisher.

Printed and bound in Canada.

VISIT US AT

 dundurn.com | 🐦 @dundurnpress | f dundurnpress | 📷 dundurnpress

Dundurn
3 Church Street, Suite 500
Toronto, Ontario, Canada
M5E 1M2

LIVING UP TO A LEGEND

LIVING UP TO A LEGEND

MY ADVENTURES
WITH BILLY BISHOP'S GHOST

DIANA BISHOP

DUNDURN
TORONTO

To our heroes, wherever we may find them

CONTENTS

ACKNOWLEDGEMENTS

During this project, I discovered that it takes a village to write a book, especially a memoir about one's life, in which so many people play a part. Whether it was to cheer me on, add constructive criticism, steer me toward deeper insight, jog my memory, or just listen to me talk endlessly about my progress, a large network of extraordinary people made it all possible. I was blessed, and I will always feel indebted.

I would like to thank the following for helping me shape my story and see my life with enriched perspective, and for walking with me on this most rewarding journey: freelance editor Barbara Berson, who got me started and helped me turn the few childhood stories I was writing into a full manuscript; my literary agent, Bill Hanna, who, coincidentally, was also my father's agent, knew and loved Dad, and reassured me that I was rendering a balanced portrait of a supremely talented yet complicated man.

Without Kirk Howard and the highly professional team at Dundurn, my memoir would never have seen the light of day, and for this I owe a debt of gratitude, especially to Sheila Douglas, who took a chance on me, and my editor Allison Hirst, copy editor Kate Unrau, and publicist Jaclyn Hodsdon.

I would also like to thank freelance designer Corey Kilmartin, who understood my vision and created the cover design for the book.

On the personal side of things, there were my many dear friends, of which I am fortunate to have more than my fair share. Shardie Stevenson and Elizabeth (Lizzie) Gilbert know me better than anyone else on this earth, and they stood by me every step of the way. Quite simply, without their devotion, consistent urging, and inspiration, I could never have done this.

I also want to thank the following people for being there for me whenever I needed them: Norman Sobel, Hope McFall, Christine Kowal, Mary Lu Toms, Jocelyn Minton, Karen Trimble, Kelly Burnett, Olga Marsenic, Charlotte deHeinrich, Harold Rees, Cathleen Colehour, Elena Georgiadou, Thomas Pratt, Pierre Marchand, Andrea Wilson, Drew Simmie, Heather Huber, Carol Deacon, Catherine Macnaughton, Dr. Joe Smolders, and Dr. Anna Lisa Reisman.

Then, of course, there is my family. Thank you all so much for supporting me through what I fully appreciate was sometimes an uneasy process. My cousins Catherine (Twink) Willis-O'Connor and Maggie Sutrov emboldened me to tell my story because they recognized that, in part, it was their story, too. And I also want to thank my brother, Bill Bishop, my sister-in-law Dr. Ginny McFarlane, my nephew Douglas Bishop, and my niece Robin Schulman. I love you all very much.

A heartfelt thanks to the compassionate staff at Kensington Gardens Health Centre who took such wonderful care of Dad at the end of his life, with a special mention to Kathy Lashley, Nuno DaSilva, Blossom Johnson, and volunteer Joseph Sengco, a young man who shared my father's passion for Canada's military history.

Finally, I want to thank all of those who serve and have served our country. My family instilled in me a deep respect for the sacrifices you make. You are all heroes to me.

PROLOGUE

On November 10, 2010, the night before Remembrance Day, my father called me.

"Hello, *helloooo*. Are you there?" he bellowed into the receiver. At eighty-seven Dad was going deaf, and he thought everyone else was, too.

"I am here, Dad, but it's 9:30 at night. Is anything wrong?" I asked, raising my voice a little to make sure I didn't have to repeat myself. I was already in bed reading, but with an aging father in a nursing home, a late-night phone call always put me on edge. Normally, Dad would be fast asleep at this hour. Tonight he sounded as though he was on high alert.

"No, no, nothing wrong," Dad chimed. "Just wanted to call and let you know that I got myself all dressed in my suit. I have put my medals on and am ready to go."

Now I was confused. What was he talking about? My first thought was that he was giving himself a little dress rehearsal for tomorrow's activities. After recent eye and dental surgery, the only Remembrance Day service and speech for which my father could summon the strength was the one he intended to give at breakfast to a room full of sedate nursing home "inmates," as he'd dubbed them.

"Yes, sir, I am going to show these peasants what Canada is all about."

My father had grown up in a world where, as he put it, "God is an Englishman" — quite different from the socially and ethnically diverse population he lived with at the nursing home — even if it was called Kensington Gardens after the Royal Park in London.

I knew that the thought of having the floor in the nursing home's dining room, however brief and unsolicited the moment would be, was still enough for my dad to dress up proudly with his medals — a symbol of his most glorious era — above his heart, and, of course, to remind all of us who he was. But Dad needed no rehearsal. He had attended so many Remembrance Day ceremonies in his lifetime that I knew he had it all down pat.

Did he plan to sleep in his clothes so that he would be ready to go in the morning? In his old age, Dad often fretted that he might sleep in and miss something — hard to imagine, as he was still the nervous ball of energy that he had always been.

My biggest worry whenever my father called was that I might have to get up, get dressed, and go over to see him. My presence was often the only thing that would calm him down. Despite my complex relationship with him over the years, I had an unwavering sense of duty to my father. I felt it was my responsibility to step in and take care of him after my mother died. I was Daddy's girl, loyal to a fault.

I was trying to formulate some response when Dad boomed, "Got to go. I have to get to the dining room before breakfast is over."

Click.

In that moment, as Dad hung up and left me on the line, holding nothing but silence, it hit me: my father was leaving me, bit by bit. I knew it; I had known it for some time. And yet that moment stunned me, stung me, and wrenched at my heart.

My whole life I had watched my father, Arthur Bishop, the only son of Canada's and the Commonwealth's most famous First World War flying ace, step up to various podiums around the country on Remembrance Day. A former fighter pilot himself, flying Spitfires in the Second World War, Dad was invited to scores of military and aviation events, and he revelled in his stardom at each show. He was masterful, playing a part that he had been born into — though it was not one he had selected for himself.

On many of these occasions, he told a captive audience that, between them, he and his father had shot down seventy-three German planes. "My father shot down seventy-two, and I shot down one!" Dad would proudly joke.

I can't recall the first time I heard Dad use that line. Like so many stories about my grandfather and my father, it felt as if I had always known them.

I do remember that Dad always delivered the quip with a wonderful mix of humility, pride, and humour that people loved.

Of course, it was a joke that masked a difficult truth for my father: he had grown up as the son of Billy Bishop, a legend, a Canadian icon. Dad had a lot to live up to.

In fact, his father's mythical status had only grown over the years. There were books, documentaries, and a highly acclaimed play about him. There were also stamps bearing his image, as well as streets, bars, cafés, an air force building, a museum, a mountain in the Canadian Rockies, and a couple of airports named after him.

I admit readily that it took me a long time to fully appreciate both the blessing and the burden that my father carried around with the Bishop name. Children only have their own experiences to rely on, and my experiences with Dad as a youngster were something of a roller coaster ride. Although there were things about him that were quite wonderful, there were many others that were awful. I battled internally and at considerable emotional cost trying to reconcile these two sides of his character because, more than anything else, I so desperately wanted my father to be a hero to me like my grandfather was.

On the one hand, he was a very funny man. Everyone thought so. Dad could walk into a room and have everyone laughing in no time. He was endowed with the perfect sense of timing, and he could really tell a joke. In fact, I was convinced he was the one who came up with new jokes — usually dirty ones — because he was always the first to tell them before they made the rounds.

Dad was always full of surprises. You never knew what he might do out of the blue, but you knew it would have you in stitches. He could give everyone real belly laughs — once at a resort Dad got up when they were playing Mexican music. He was in his mid-fifties by then, but he took the floor in front of a large dinner crowd to do the most energetic hat dance you have ever seen. As the music got more intense, so did Dad's dancing. Ten minutes later he was still at it, with the crowd cheering and madly clapping. I was convinced he was headed for a heart attack, but no, he went on and on until the music finally stopped. He ended his big solo by taking a bow.

All his life my father had been wiry and compact, with unbridled vivacity; you could almost see sparks flying off of him in all directions. Surprisingly, dementia had not taken away that fire in his belly or the twinkle in his eye, but his body had diminished, a much tinier version of its former self. In casual and sports clothes Dad had always looked messy, but in a suit and tie he could really put it together — a bit of a metaphor for his life in general, or so it seemed to me.

As I held the phone, I knew Dad would be drowning in his navy-blue suit jacket. But my heart burst with respect, knowing that he would have expertly knotted his tie with the tiny Spitfires all over it. He would have remembered to wear a deep red poppy, the familiar emblem of Remembrance Day, and his breastplate of war medals would be in place over his heart.

I imagined him determinedly working his way down the long hallway of the nursing home using his walker and arriving at the dining hall, perplexed to find it dark and empty — it was 9:30 at night, after all. That was if he even made it that far; it's likely the evening nursing attendant would be surprised to see him up and dressed at that hour, and, as diplomatically as possible, would try to coax him back to bed. There would probably be quite a scene.

It was at that moment that I felt an overwhelming sense of panic. I knew that my father would not be here much longer, and I needed to face the facts: For all my devotion to him, particularly in his waning years, I had spent much of my life not only struggling to understand this larger-than-life force that was my father but also trying to resolve my own complicated feelings about him, feelings that had burdened me my entire life. I had to reconcile the fact that a man who could do a Mexican hat dance long enough for a Guinness World Record and keep a room full of people in stitches could also be so very cruel to those closest to him.

I felt I needed to understand more deeply the forces that shaped my father's life and, ultimately, my own. Not surprisingly, it all seemed to lead back to my famous grandfather.

Our Billy Bishop was not just Canada's war hero; he was our hero, too. As his family, we worshipped him — who he was, what he did, what he stood for — even when it didn't always make a lot of sense. Billy certainly wasn't perfect, yet we still held tight to our unshakeable super-human image of him. In fact, there is no doubt in my mind that Billy Bishop has been one of greatest influences in my life, propelling me to be adventurous and courageous, but also haunting me to try too hard, be too hard on myself, and feel like I could never measure up. That impact is what I needed and wanted to understand better.

I think we all struggle to find ourselves in our family narrative. I certainly did, realizing that, like my father, I had grown up feeling that I must live up to a legend. When I think about the years I spent as a journalist, telling other people's stories, and then as a communications and branding specialist, helping people to tell their own stories, I understand that all along I have been searching for a way to tell my own story.

These are the factors that sparked this journey to explore the forces that were unleashed with my proud military heritage and the impact it has had on my life and my family's life because living with the memory of Billy Bishop has been like living with a ghost — a friendly ghost, yes, but one that has always been there with us in spirit, shaping our lives in particular ways, and challenging me to contemplate *what is a hero*? And what role do heroes play in our lives?

CHAPTER 1

BILLY AND ME

Believe me, there would have had to be a very good reason for me to go rummaging through my father's underwear drawer — if you ever saw the sorry state of my father's underwear, it would speak for itself. Believe it or not, though, that drawer was, for many years, where my family kept my grandfather's impressive breastplate of First World War medals, now considered some of the most valuable on the planet. In a sense, the underwear drawer is where my relationship with my famous grandfather truly began.

Before digging through the armoire, all I knew about Billy Bishop was what my parents had told me because, sadly, my Grandpa Billy had died when he was just sixty-two. I had been three years old at the time, too young to have any memory of him.

My father tried to appease me with statements like "You were the only baby that your grandfather ever held in his arms." This only caused me to jump to a number of unsettling conclusions: That my grandfather was not fond of babies. That he had never held my father as a baby. Or that my parents were just saying this to make up for the fact that I would never know him. I hoped that the latter was true.

"When Billy came over for lunch, he would often take a nap afterwards in the guest bedroom and wanted you to sleep in your crib next to him," my mother added.

Dad said Billy had a special name for me: "the Boobit."

Why the Boobit, you may ask. Well, it just sounded cute, and my family was always giving people silly names.

The way everyone talked about Billy, though, it was clear he was a god in our family, so I figured that even if I couldn't see him, Grandpa Billy was always around — like a ghost hiding in the house.

The idea of ghosts seemed normal to me as a child. I would walk into a room or wake up in the middle of the night and feel something filling the space around me. Where the air usually felt light, I could stretch my hands out and feel a fullness or density, which I assumed was something or some-*one* passing by from the invisible world. I was sensitive like that, and it didn't scare me. In fact, I found it comforting to think there was so much going on that we couldn't see. It seemed rational to me that even if I could not actually see my grandfather, he was there and always would be — an otherworldly presence to remind me who I am and where I came from.

This phenomenon really came into focus when I was ten years old and in grade five. I remember putting on a pretty dress one day (probably pink because that was my favourite colour). I had wanted to make sure I looked my absolute best that morning.

My father always dashed off to work early, well before I left for school, so I waited for him to leave; then, while my mother was busy cleaning up the dishes downstairs, I snuck back upstairs into Dad's den. I had been planning this for a while and was virtually buzzing with anticipation as I opened Dad's armoire and that underwear drawer I had visited so many times without his knowledge.

My right hand rummaged through the mishmash of socks, undershirts, and briefs until I finally felt the breastplate, which I carefully pulled out, holding it flat, and placed in a brown paper bag. I was careful to wrap the paper around the breastplate, and then I tucked the package securely under my arm.

My school was only two blocks away — a good thing under the circumstances. I felt as if I had stolen the family jewels and that, at any moment, someone might come chasing after me. My father had given my brother and me strict orders never to touch this precious item except when he was around, an order which, being kids, we ignored, sneaking our friends up to look at them every chance we got. I don't remember my father ever saying I couldn't take them to school, but it was too late at that point to consider the consequences.

Once I got to school, I put the paper bag on top of my desk and kept my hands firmly over it. I couldn't wait for my name to be called. I knew my classmates would never guess the remarkable treasure that I had brought to show them.

Fame is a funny thing. If you have it in your family, it can rub off on you. You can feel a little bit famous even if you've done nothing to earn it. I certainly did that day.

When I was a child, it didn't seem all that surprising to me that my grandfather's impressive breastplate of war medals — fifteen in all — were kept in my father's underwear drawer. It never occurred to me to ask my dad why he kept them hidden away. I surmise that, at the time, he thought it was as safe a place as any. Little did he know …

My class already knew something of Billy Bishop, the war hero, as his name had come up in one of our history lessons in the months before. The teacher had asked us to open our books to a particular page, and there, in the top left-hand corner, was a close-up of a dashing pilot in the cockpit of his plane.

Billy Bishop, my grandfather, First World War flying ace, in his Nieuport 17. No. 60 Squadron RFC, Filescamp Farm, 1917.

The right side of my grandfather's face was turned slightly toward the camera, a crinkle at the corner of his eye, just as I would have in the corner of my eyes when I got a little older. The photo was in black and white, but from the brightness and intensity in those eyes, you knew they were a brilliant blue.

Under the picture was the caption — *World War I Flying Ace, Billy Bishop!* It felt as if my heart leapt out of my chest. I turned to my closest classmate and whispered loudly, "That's Billy Bishop, my grandfather. MY grandfather!"

The teacher had pointed out the picture to the class and mentioned that I was his granddaughter. It was so unexpected that I just beamed. That's when I decided that I wouldn't keep my grandfather's medals hidden the way my father did, and had taken the risk of sneaking them out of their hiding place and carting them off to school as the highlight of my history project.

When I stood before my class and pulled out my unique show and tell, my classmates did not disappoint, especially the boys. Their eyes opened wide as I laid out Billy Bishop's legacy — a tapestry of different medals — some shiny, some dull, some silver, gold, and bronze. Each one was attached to a colourful ribbon and arranged one slightly over top of the next in a long, neat row.

I had painstakingly memorized them so that I could confidently name some of them: the Distinguished Service Order; the Military Cross; the Distinguished Flying Cross; the Croix de Guerre; the Legion of Honour; and the most coveted of all, the Victoria Cross, the highest military decoration awarded for valour in the face of the enemy. That one was first on the breastplate, standing out in its elegant simplicity — a dark bronze cross crafted from metal harvested from guns from the Crimean War, hanging from a richly ribbed maroon ribbon.

Emboldened by my powerful prop, I began to tell my class about my Grandfather Billy. I had reread my history book the night before to make sure that I got everything right, but having listened to my family talk about him so often, I knew all the salient points anyway.

"My grandfather got these for his courage and because he shot down seventy-two planes in the First World War," I began. "My grandfather was awarded the top medal for bravery." I pointed out the VC on the breastplate. I took a breath and carried on. "It isn't as shiny as the others, but it is very special. Very few people in the war ever got one."

Billy Bishop (centre) speaks with King George V, Windsor Park, 1918.

Ploughing on, I said, "The King of England presented it to my grandfather for attacking a German aerodrome and shooting down a bunch of enemy planes. Nobody had ever done that before!"

Once I had finished, my classmates were eager to see the war medals up close. I couldn't have been more thrilled to have them stand around me as they traced their fingertips over each of them, as I had done so many times, savouring every indentation as if trying to feel Billy's presence.

When the questions started, I was ready.

"Who was Billy's archrival?"

"The Red Baron!" I exclaimed enthusiastically, as I knew my class had probably heard about the German ace — I was hoping nobody would ask me to pronounce his real name, Manfred Von Richthofen, though. "He was the top-scoring pilot of World War One, who shot down eighty planes."

"Did your grandfather ever fight the Red Baron?" another of my classmates asked.

"Yes, but they were both such good fighters that neither was able to shoot the other down," I replied.*

A few years later, when kids would ask me this same question, I was able to add "My grandfather was like Snoopy," knowing everyone was by then familiar with Charles Shultz's *Peanuts* comic strip that portrayed Snoopy the dog as a First World War pilot, adorned with goggles and a white scarf and taking on the German flying ace from atop his doghouse. Except that, I pointed out, my grandfather didn't like to wear goggles; he insisted he could see better without them.

The last question a classmate asked me that day was "Did you know your grandfather? What was he like?"

Of course, I had to tell them that I didn't know him, but it left so much unsaid. How could I tell them that Billy Bishop was all around me? That I considered him my own personal superhero, one of the good guys who, I believed, watched over me — not to mention dashing and handsome like a movie star (Canadian writer Pierre Berton once said that Billy Bishop had the face of Paul Newman and the body of James Cagney).

I delighted in poring over our family photographs of Billy, most of which were kept in a couple of worn albums — the old-fashioned ones with the black pages in which black-and-white pictures were held in place by those maddening little corner flaps. We had originals of the official war photos of my grandfather that are now part of the public domain — Billy posing in the cockpit of his First World War biplane, aiming his Lewis gun into the heavens. But the albums also contained Billy the toddler (or "Willie" as they called him then), dressed in a sailor's outfit of the kind that many parents forced their kids to wear in those days; and later, the elegant man dressed in the latest tailored suit from Savile Row in London, playing polo with dignitaries and visiting Winston Churchill at 10 Downing Street. I followed Billy's life in these pictures. They have such liveliness about them that you almost feel he might suddenly wink at you from the photo.

Billy's legend was central to our family's life. Stories about him were the enthralling highlight of most gatherings. So many stories, told so often as to become lore, and I cherished them.

---

* This is what I believed to be true from our family lore. Billy had penned in his autobiography, *Winged Warfare*, that he had once encountered the Red Baron in a dogfight; however, some historians have questioned the encounter, and there is no corroborating record of it.

Billy and British prime minister Winston Churchill at 10 Downing Street, 1940.

One memorable war story in my father's arsenal was about the bullet that grazed his father's temple as he was up shooting at the Germans. As a souvenir of this nearly fatal shot, Billy had kept the windshield of the plane with the bullet hole in it, and Dad displayed it rather proudly in his den. (I impressed my friends by telling them that if the bullet had strayed an inch to the right, I would not be here to tell the tale.)

Frankly, I was still too young to appreciate my grandfather's war exploits and the endless stream of battles that had made him a legend. Instead, I preferred hearing the entertaining anecdotes about a man who always went out of his way to inject a little more fun into everyone's lives.

My dad was the family chronicler of his father's life. He had written Billy's biography, a bestseller entitled *The Courage of the Early Morning*, named for my grandfather's trademark habit of going out to face the enemy alone at first light. While the book had primarily focused on the drama in the air, there were also the stories about Billy the family man, the bon vivant, and the prankster, and my dad would regale us with these often. The tales about Billy kept him alive for all of us.

One of my favourite yarns was about the time Billy hosted a dinner party for a large table of well-heeled guests where everything was served backwards. The dinner started with coffee, then dessert, and so on, finishing with cocktails. Even the servers came into the room backwards. I always thought it would be fun to try that myself.

My grandfather was also very fond of dogs. Dad told me Billy liked chow chows — those fluffy Chinese dogs that look like lions — so once, during another dinner party, he placed two of them as a centrepiece in the middle of the table.

"How did he ever get them to stay there?" I asked when I heard this story for the first time.

"He just had a way with them," was the reply I got.

I needed no further convincing that my grandfather had been no ordinary human being when my Granny Bishop, Billy's widow, told me why Billy never wore a watch. He couldn't, she said, because whenever he did, within a short period of time the hands would start going backwards, speed up, and the watch would stop. Some believe it happens to people who have a strong magnetic field or electric current around them.

It was also my grandmother who described Billy to me as a flame that blazed so strongly that it sucked every bit of oxygen out of the room, and while I was never exactly sure what she meant by that, it also seemed an appropriate description of my father. When Dad was in the room, it was difficult to focus on anything or anyone else. He was constantly on, feeling a need to perform, whether it was before an audience of one or of many.

I sometimes imagined when I entered a room that Billy might have been there, and I had just missed him. Once or twice I even tried to see if I could contact his spirit. The Ouija board seemed a good way to give that a try. I gingerly placed my fingertips on the heart-shaped piece of wood used to communicate with the spirits and asked the board the obvious question.

"Is my grandfather Billy Bishop here?"

On the top of the Ouija board are two rows set in a semicircle that contain the letters of the alphabet. This allows anyone on the other side to spell out a message. But the words "yes" and "no" also appear on the top corners.

Just in case he might not have heard me the first time, I said, "Billy, it's me, your granddaughter, Diana … the Boobit. Are you there?"

My young and impressionable self would have taken any movement toward "yes" as a clear sign of his intent to contact me. That's when my hands started to tingle. Or maybe I just imagined it.

I waited....

Nothing.

A very serious — and decidedly
"ghostly" — portrait of Billy, 1918.

And so I made a trip back to my father's underwear drawer to sneak another look at my grandfather's medals, an activity that always made me feel close to him. They were heavy in my small hands. They felt powerful, important.

I did get the medals back home safe and sound the day I took them to school — back into the underwear drawer.* My father kept his own medals — a more modest collection, to be sure — in a desk drawer in his den. But he never talked with us, at least not when I was a child, about his own war experiences. He talked only of Billy's achievements, which were recounted almost like fairy tales, stories about our family's shining first knight of the air.

Thankfully, my father had been at work all day and hadn't noticed Billy's medals were missing. I likely would have gotten into some serious trouble if he had, but it would have been worth it.

From that day forward Billy Bishop became a big part of my identity. I would hear the kids at school whisper when I passed in the hall — "Do you know who her grandfather was? Billy Bishop, the First World War flying

---

* A few years later, believing that his father's medals belonged to all Canadians, my father had the good sense to donate them to the Canadian War Museum in Ottawa, where they are on display. I am told they are insured for several million dollars.

ace!" I saw how they looked at me afterwards. I felt special, but also as if something more would always be expected of me. I stood a little taller and straighter, hopeful that Billy hovered nearby, watching over all of us — but especially over me. I needed a superhero, someone to make me feel proud, and within whose protective aura I could feel safe.

CHAPTER 2

SON OF A WAR HERO

In a way, my birth was a bit of a miracle. My mother loved to tell me over and over again that when she first held me in her arms, she looked into my eyes and saw the person who would become her best friend. That story never failed to touch me because it was so true.

My mother wanted children more than anything in the world. But it wasn't easy for her. My parents had been married almost eight years by the time I finally arrived.

My mother had suffered a series of miscarriages and a stillbirth — the circumstances around which were very sad indeed: Eight months pregnant with only a week or two to go before her delivery date, my mother had gone to her obstetrician feeling uneasy. A fetal exam could discern no heartbeat. After so many failed pregnancies, the baby that had grown for nearly nine months inside my mother's womb, and was so close to taking its first breath, had died.

Perhaps even more tragic was that my mother would have to deliver the stillborn. That meant waiting until she went into labour. And so she went home to wait — alone. My father wasn't there because he had hurt his back and was in the hospital with orders for complete bed rest.

My grandparents, Billy and Margaret, had stepped in — insisting that my mother stay with them until she felt the first labour pains. They kept my mother's spirits up during that terrible week, and when the contractions began, it was Billy who drove her to the hospital.

As my mother remembered it, "Your grandfather got me in the car and started telling me stories. Looking back, even now, I find this hard to believe myself — but we started chattering about some of the funny things he had done."

After one of my mother's previous miscarriages, Billy had arrived at my parent's apartment, where Granny Bishop and a neighbour were keeping my mother company. Before knocking on the door, Billy had taken off all his clothes out in the hallway — leaving only his top hat, a tie around his neck, and his cane, and exposing his middle-aged pot belly.

"Can you picture it? Billy sporting a big smile as my grandmother opened the door — and then the surprise when he realized she wasn't alone. Your grandfather had me laughing all the way to the delivery room," my mother recalled with obvious admiration, as if she, too, had found her superhero.

My mother gave birth to a boy that day, perfect in every way except that he was dead. I don't think they buried him because I don't know of any grave. My father was in the same hospital at the same time my mother gave birth, but on a different floor, one floor above. He was able to keep in touch by telephone, but Dad said he was still so wracked with pain he couldn't leave his bed.

I always found that part of the story hard to understand, but my mother said Dad had been a nervous wreck since the war, and she intimated that the tragic news about the baby was too much for him. My father, on the other hand, told me that he had felt terrible that he could not be there to comfort her. There is such an obvious disconnect in the differing versions of their stories, and I remember it being one of my earliest recollections that there could be different truths, unspoken truths, between my parents.

*   *   *

My parents met as teenagers. My mother had many suitors, one in particular that she liked — a young man named Walt who was eventually shot down during the war. I was still pretty young, about seven, when Mom first showed me pictures in her photo album of the handsome young Royal Canadian Air Force pilot. Smiling, she recalled how Dad would wince whenever she

"She was simply the most beautiful girl I ever saw," Dad recalled. Mom and Dad sharing a drink at Standish Hall in Hull, Quebec, 1944.

mentioned Walt's name. She enjoyed teasing my father. From the start, he had made it clear to her that there had never been anyone else for him — not since he had first spied my mother at a dance: she was just fifteen years old and wearing a very grown-up chartreuse-coloured cocktail dress.

"She was simply the most beautiful girl I ever saw," Dad recalled. Many people would have agreed. My mother was a knockout, an Ottawa golden girl who caught the eye of renowned photographer Yousuf Karsh. She was photographed often by him, and at the time my mother became engaged to my father, Karsh's storefront window prominently displayed a large portrait of my mother, arms crossed, her long dark hair cascading down her back as she leaned slightly to the left.

Billy was wasting his breath, but initially he advised my father to allow for other considerations in finding a suitable wife. Billy encouraged him to marry for money because, of course, that's what he'd done, marrying into the Eaton family — although as it turned out, he also married the woman he loved. My grandmother, Margaret Beattie (her mother's maiden name)

My grandparents, Billy and Margaret, looking very stylish in the Roaring Twenties.

Eaton Burden, was the granddaughter of Timothy Eaton, whose legacy was the Canadian national department store chain, founded in 1869. And in Canada, especially at that time, the Eatons were homegrown royalty that often drew comparisons with the Kennedys in the United States.

Billy was keen for his son to marry into a family of similar economic standing and status.

"The old man wanted me to marry Katherine Kemp, the daughter of Sir Edward Kemp," Dad said. Kemp was a contemporary of Billy's, had been a successful businessman and politician — both as Canada's Minister of Militia and Defence and as Minister of Overseas Military Forces during the First World War — and, therefore, his daughter would have both money and stature.

Marrying royalty would have been even better. Billy somehow had a hand in an article in one of the New York tabloids where my father was included as a possible suitor for Princess Elizabeth, the future Queen of England!

When the article appeared, Dad was still overseas, flying missions over France, and it was Billy who broke the news to my father in a telegram.

> CONGRATS SON, STOP.
> IF YOU ARE FOLLOWING THE PAPERS, STOP.
> RESERVE A WING IN BUCKINGHAM PALACE WITH HOT
> AND COLD CHAMBERMAIDS, STOP.

However, Billy's efforts had little impact on my father, who had grown more besotted with Priscilla ("Cilla") Aylen, the dark-haired beauty from a prominent and well-off (although not as rich as Billy would have liked) Ottawa family.

Mom's upbringing had been privileged in its own way. Jack and Jean Aylen were established, cultured, and highly respected Ottawa nobility. Cilla's father was an esteemed bilingual lawyer, a Queen's Counsel who was educated at Harvard and had studied civil law at the Université de Montréal. My grandmother was also highly accomplished, having been the first female chairperson of the trustees of the Ottawa Civic Hospital. She had also been named Ottawa Citizen of the Year for her many other non-profit and philanthropic endeavours. "An Ottawa woman shoulders one of the capital's largest volunteer jobs and does it without neglecting her lawyer-husband or her weekly shopping," wrote the *Ottawa Citizen*.[*]

While the Aylens were very social people and great patrons of the arts, especially theatre, their overall demeanour was humble, unassuming, and modest. For my mother, they must have been a sharp contrast to the more flamboyant and self-important Bishops. To her, my father, the son of a war hero, seemed like quite the catch.

---

* "Hospital Board Chairman Leads Busy Active Life," *Ottawa Citizen*, March 7, 1956.

* * *

My father was born on Friday, June 13, 1923, and was named Arthur Christian William Avery Bishop, after Prince Arthur, the Duke of Connaught (and son of Queen Victoria), who became my dad's godfather.

I know so little of my father's childhood except for the photos of him that bear strong evidence of his regal beginnings. Two in particular stand out for me: In one Dad is about three or four years of age, standing in a silk dressing gown, his thick blond curls circling an angelic face and impish grin. In the other he and his younger sister, Margaret Marise (nicknamed "Jackie" after a beloved dog, apparently), were dressed in Christian Dior and standing beside their ponies.

I would spend hours staring at these photos, thinking that if I looked at them long enough, I might be able to recognize in this aristocrat the less-than-genteel man I knew as my father and to somehow reconcile the two.

After the war Billy had become an international celebrity. His heroic exploits as a fighter pilot were well-known, and he'd authored a book about them called *Winged Warfare*, which became an instant success and heightened his demand on the speakers' circuit, filling packed houses, such as New York's Carnegie Hall. As he had been the first of a breed to do combat in the air, I imagined how thrilling it would have been to hear my grandfather recount, in his own words, what it was like to climb into those first rickety marvels of aviation to fly out in search of the enemy.

When he wasn't speaking about aerial warfare, my grandfather tried his hand at business, establishing a short-lived passenger air service along with Billy Barker, a fellow Canadian and Victoria Cross winner. The business eventually failed when it ran into financial difficulties, but my father told me it had never been too serious a venture, anyway, set up mostly so that Billy could fly his friends up to their cottages on the Muskokan lakes north of Toronto.

In 1921 Billy and Margaret moved to London, England, where Billy had secured a couple of lucrative positions, one of which with a company that had developed a new method for producing iron pipe and wanted to capitalize on my grandfather's widespread connections. It was there that my father and aunt were born. For the first six years of my father's life, he and his sister lived in a Tudor-style house near stylish Regent's Park, where Billy made the most of his status as a war hero and his upper-crust contacts.

A dapper-looking Billy Bishop (left). He spent his time in London hobnobbing with celebrities and royals.

While he acquired quite a considerable fortune, Billy spent it just as quickly on a lavish lifestyle, being chauffeured around in a Rolls-Royce, hobnobbing with royalty, and vacationing in the south of France, while mingling with the likes of Ernest Hemingway, Scott and Zelda Fitzgerald, and the Prince of Wales (later King Edward VIII). And anyway, if things didn't work out, Billy always had my grandmother's money to fall back on.

My grandmother had grown up in luxurious surroundings as part of the illustrious Eaton clan in Toronto. She had studied at the Ontario College of Art but was never skilled or even interested in the domestic arts. She was certainly not a homemaker, so my father and his sister were primarily brought up by nannies and then shipped off to boarding school when they were old enough. With their father's busy life, neither of them saw him all that often, and they likely didn't see much of their mother either.

Dad grew up idolizing his father and enjoyed, for the most part, the many comparisons people began to make about father and son. For one thing, they looked a lot alike. Both were compact, sturdy, and intense, with those clear blue eyes. My dad, when he was old enough, cultivated that resemblance, growing a moustache just like his father's.

If anyone looked closely, though, they would have noticed that Dad's features were just a tad coarser than Billy's. Billy had an aquiline nose, or at least he started out with one — as a civilian, he broke it crash-landing a plane. Billy was otherwise unhurt, but his nose never healed to its original state. Dad's nose was more prominent and made a stronger statement.

Billy was a bit of a dandy, who turned up frequently on best-dressed lists. He paid meticulous attention to his attire, whether it was wearing his uniform or his expensively tailored civilian clothes. His suits and shoes were handmade; even his ties were cut specially for him. Conversely, my father often took pleasure in looking like an unmade bed. In his casual clothes, and even in his off-duty war photos, Dad liked to look scrappy. These were minor differences, however, because in almost every other way my father wanted to be just like his father.

I never heard Dad once complain about the obvious — that his father cast a long shadow. He had gone off to boarding school at an early age, but he told me he'd had a pretty hard time there because a particularly sadistic headmaster beat him regularly and chided him with comments like "You think you are a big deal, eh, being Billy Bishop's son?"

The comparisons magnified during the Second World War after my father enlisted. He joined the Royal Canadian Air Force in 1941 at the age of eighteen to become a fighter pilot, just like his dad. The whole world — at least all of Canada — was watching the son who dared to follow in his famous father's footsteps. When my father headed to Canadian

Forces Base Uplands in Ottawa for Service Flying Training School, the *Montreal Gazette* ran a story with the following quote: "He has the greatest name in military aviation to live up to."

Despite his admiration for, even worship of, his father, I suspect that there were times he wished he could escape the weight of his father's fame.

*   *   *

My father began courting my mother in earnest after the war when the couple enjoyed riding the coattails of Billy and Margaret's lifestyle.

At the time, my grandparents lived in a large house at the corner of Blackburn and Laurier Avenues, a block from Prime Minister Mackenzie King's house in the nation's capital. It was a lovely old turn-of-the-century Ottawa homestead, warmed with stained-glass windows, oak wainscotting, a majestic staircase, three floors of sprawling rooms, and a very large veranda that wrapped around the back of the house. It was a natural venue for grand parties and barbecues with a wide array of dignitaries and celebrities flowing through — all of which must have been very exciting for Arthur and Priscilla, who were getting to know each other better.

In August 1944 my father had barely been home a month from overseas when he took up a post with the photographic wing at the RCAF Station Rockcliffe. With the overall intention of doing aerial survey work in Canada's north, the squadron was set up primarily to begin training on the various aircraft and to do some practice flights. Billy had encouraged Dad to take the position until something better turned up, and my father told me he only agreed to the job because the squadron had two of his beloved Spitfires, the type of plane Dad flew in the war.

"It was pretty tame work after everything I had been through, and it almost made me miss being shot at — almost!" Dad quipped.

In addition to this posting, Billy had also arranged for my father to be his aide-de-camp (ADC), or personal assistant, as Billy was then air marshal and director of the Royal Canadian Air Force. It meant that Dad would often accompany Billy on official business.

Billy and Arthur pose together wearing their Air Force uniforms, 1945.

My mother was concerned. She felt that Dad was burnt-out from having flown over one hundred missions during the war and Billy was rushing things.

"Your father was still a bundle of nerves and needed time to relax," my mother recalled.

But my grandfather did not share this view because, frankly, that's not how he had done things. Even between his tours as a fighter pilot in France (between the fall of 1917 and the spring of 1918), Billy had returned to Canada a hero, married Margaret, and authored his book. After the war, Billy immediately went on a speaking tour and then dove into the world of business. There was no time to decompress or to let his thoughts or war experiences catch up with him. And perhaps that's how so many of his generation managed to keep going after all that they had been through.

Billy must have also felt this was the best strategy for his son because, before long, he had made new career plans for my father. On official business together in Windsor, Ontario, Billy announced to my father that they would be having lunch with the owner of the *Windsor Daily Star*, who had supported the RCAF recruitment effort that Billy had spearheaded. A few weeks later, out of the blue and without rhyme or reason, Billy asked my father how he might like a job as a reporter.

Billy Bishop presents my father with his wings during the Second World War. My father would go on to fly Spitfires, serving with No. 401 Squadron RCAF in 1943–44.

Dad was less than enthusiastic about the idea to start with, but changed his tune when he was connected (most definitely Billy had a hand in this, too) with the seasoned freelance newsman Cornelius "Neil" Vanderbilt IV, a renegade of the American blueblood family who had made history in bringing back the first film footage of Hitler's rise to supremacy and the subjugation of the Jews. Dad was enthralled with Vanderbilt's stories and suddenly considered that journalism might offer some of the adventure he had been missing.

So Windsor was where my parents started out their married life. After honeymooning in New York (a present from my grandparents), where they lived it up at the Ritz-Carlton, Arthur and Cilla arrived at their new home — a dingy apartment that cost twenty-five dollars a month and was in dire need of a thorough cleaning. My father plunged into his life as a reporter, learning a new trade while my mother sat down and had a good cry before she scrubbed the place from top to bottom.

"From the Ritz and the Stork Club to 30 Pitt Street. Quite the experience, let me tell you!" Mom recalled about their arrival in Windsor.

With the late-night newspaper deadlines, my father usually didn't come home until almost midnight after having imbibed a few with the boys at the office. There he would find my mother trying to keep the meal hot and the ice cold, but ready to snap to attention and play the part of devoted wife as they talked for hours over more drinks. Finally, they would both collapse into bed around four or five in the morning, only to repeat the process all over again the next day.

"We were young. It was fun in those days," she told me.

As things turned out, my father's journalism career, while rewarding, was brief: rewarding because it was as a reporter that Dad found a passion for writing that would serve him well; brief because, within a year and a few months of acquiring the job, Dad was offered a new opportunity — this one with Ronalds Advertising Agency in Montreal. This, too, had come to him through his father. Billy had recently retired as air marshal and took up a previously held position as vice president of McColl-Frontenac Oil (which eventually became Texaco), and it used Ronalds for their advertising.

The pay was certainly better: Dad earned $275 a month compared to the $120 he was getting as a reporter, a stronger foundation for my parents to start the next phase of their lives.

CHAPTER 3

Mom, Dad, and Us Kids

With my mother's history, the doctors didn't take any chances when she became pregnant with me. She was closely monitored, and when the due date drew closer, it was decided that I would be born via Caesarean section.

"This is actually a nicer way to be born," Mom said a little defensively, "as you didn't come into the world all crunched up and wrinkled." The other plus she professed was that she knew exactly when it would happen. The date and time of my birth was set for 9:00 a.m., Tuesday, May 19, 1953, and I arrived right on time, weighing seven pounds, two ounces, with a full head of black hair, ten fingers and toes — and screaming my head off.

My parents toyed with royal names for me like Victoria, Elizabeth, and also (and here I cringe) Heidi. I will be forever grateful that my father liked the name Diana. He said girls should have a name ending in *A* because it sounded more feminine. He also liked that Diana means "bright one," from the Latin root *di* — "to shine." I was impressed that he had put so much thought into it.

Still, Diana was not a popular choice with the grandparents, especially Granny Bishop. She expected all female offspring to be called Margaret because that was her name, her mother's name, and her grandmother's name before that. Billy's mother's name had also, coincidentally, been Margaret. It wasn't even enough for Granny that my cousin Maggie (the daughter of my Aunt Jackie, who you may recall was officially named Margaret Marise), born three weeks before me, met that fate. Billy tried to exert pressure on

Dad to follow my grandmother's wishes, but my father would not be swayed. One Margaret in my generation of the family was enough, my father said.

For four blissful years, I was an only child and quite happy about it. We lived in Montreal for the first year of my life, and then my father was promoted to vice president at the advertising firm and was transferred to Edmonton to run Ronalds' western division.

I only remember snippets of those early years, such as our house. It had a Spanish design with a red-tiled roof, and we were near the end of a cul-de-sac.

It was the fifties, long before parents obsessed about their kids' safety. So even on the coldest of winter days, my mother would pack me into my snowsuit and point me out the door to play. I'd come back for lunch, then out I would go again.

I'm not sure what I did all day, but I had a pal named Margaret (my grandmother would have been pleased), and I remember feeding some rabbits that one of the neighbours kept in a cage in their backyard. There was also an ice cream truck that came around in the summer, and I especially remember one spring day when I threw my new red galoshes down an open sewer to see what would happen. I can't remember why I wanted to do this; perhaps I was just trying my hand at being daring. I am surprised I didn't fall in, too, when they disappeared into the murky water. My mother said she was really mad, but I don't remember that; she never seemed to get mad at me. In fact, life as a four-year-old was pretty darn perfect.

And then my mother got pregnant again.

If she prepared me for the birth of my brother, I have no recollection, but his entrance into the world made quite a statement, admittedly through no fault of his own.

This was another difficult pregnancy. My parents had hired a nanny to keep me occupied so that my mother could stay off her feet with complete bed rest until the date arrived. Again a C-section was planned, but my brother was in a bit of a hurry, so things did not go as smoothly as hoped.

One morning in early April 1957, after my father had gone to work, my mother lay in her bed writhing with pain. My parents had hired a nanny to take care of me during my mother's pregnancy, and she had sent me out to play. I was on the front lawn when I heard the sirens. They seemed very far away at first, far enough away that I wouldn't have thought they were coming to our house. But they got louder and louder, and soon enough a big black car (yes, oddly, ambulances were black in Edmonton in the fifties) roared up our street and parked in the driveway. Two men in white suits got out, went to the back of the car, pulled out a stretcher, and flew by me to the front door.

By this time I was feeling my first taste of fear and panic. *What's going on? Why are they running into our house?* My heart racing, I ran after them, but as they climbed the stairs two at a time, Nanny intercepted me and told me to wait outside. It seemed like a very long time indeed — but it wasn't, only a couple of minutes or so — before the two men, one on either end of the stretcher, carried out my mother, who lay very still with her eyes closed.

Of course, I thought she was dead. My panic led to hysteria, and as my mouth caught up to my dread, I started screaming.

"Mommy, where are they taking you? Mommy, MOMMY, MOMMMMMY!"

My mother told me later that she had heard my wails, and it broke her heart to leave me there, but she was just too weak to respond.

The two men said nothing as they deftly lifted my mother into the back of the ambulance and closed the doors. As I stood sobbing, the attendants jumped back into the car and sped off down the street, the sound of sirens deafening at first and then becoming more and more distant. It was a dramatic scene for a little girl who suddenly thought she had been abandoned.

Nanny! I suddenly remembered. *Where is Nanny?*

I ran as fast as I could back into the house and up the stairs to find Nanny hurriedly stripping the bed sheets. I was so relieved to see her until, to my horror, I caught sight of the blood. It seemed to me there was so much of it. My shrill screaming overtook the scene. I simply could not comprehend what I was seeing, and I can still recall the panic I felt that day, even so many years later. It was such a defining moment, instilling in me an almost primal fear of childbirth that has never left me.

I am guessing that Nanny went to every possible length to convince me that my mother would be okay, but I have no recollection of that. My father didn't seem to be around at all. I just remember that I couldn't be consoled until my mother came home a whole week later. It didn't faze me at all that she had come home alone. They may have tried to tell me about my little brother, but I didn't hear it. I was just relieved my mother was better.

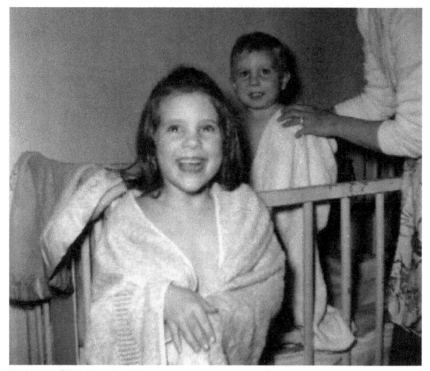

My brother Bill and me in 1958.

A few weeks later, though, my parents returned to the hospital, but this time, much to my astonishment, they came home with the newest member of the family. My brother had been born a preemie, weighing just over four pounds, and had to spend time in an incubator before being strong enough to face the world and, unwittingly, end my life as an only child.

The good news is that I thought my baby brother was the most beautiful thing I had ever seen, and I hardly ever let him out of my sight, especially in those first few days.

One night in my eagerness to keep looking at him, I pulled his bassinette over by mistake and he fell out, right onto his head. Fortunately, my little brother had a hard head and suffered no ill effects. Imagine if I had injured the only male heir to the Bishop name and lineage!

My brother was christened William Aylen (my mother's maiden name) Bishop. Unlike the name Margaret, there could never be too many Williams in our family. Sadly, our grandfather Billy had died seven months before my brother was born and never got to meet his new grandson and namesake.

CHAPTER 4

DEWAR'S ON THE ROCKS

Billy Bishop died in Florida on September 11, 1956. He was alone except for his loyal aide, Lethbridge, or "Leffo" as everyone in the family called him. Coincidentally, my grandmother was visiting us in Edmonton when it happened. At just three years of age, I was too young to go, but my father and grandmother hurried to Toronto along with my Aunt Jackie and other members of our family to take part in my grandfather's full military funeral. In fact, thirty-five thousand people turned out to pay their respects.

"Ace of Aces" and "Billy Bishop Is Dead!" screamed the newspaper headlines, as if no one could quite believe it. I guess if you had been shot at as many times as my grandfather, it must have come as quite a surprise to people that the man whom the Germans had called "Hell's Handmaiden" could simply die quietly in his sleep.

My grandfather was just sixty-two when he died, but from all the pictures we had of him in his last years, he looked twenty years older. Dad later told me that his father had aged rapidly after the First World War, partly because of the toll the war had probably taken on him, and partly because, even after the war, Billy continued to be a man of action, barely stopping to take a breath — until his last.

After the service at Timothy Eaton Memorial, the same church in which Billy and my grandmother had been married, people lined the streets for five kilometres as the funeral procession walked to the slow rhythm of muffled black drums. A young flying officer carried three rows of my grandfather's medals on a black satin pillow.

At the cemetery where my grandfather's body was cremated, two buglers played "The Last Post" and "Reveille" while twelve CF-100 jets roared low overhead in a last salute. That must have been something to see.

The *Ottawa Journal* wrote an editorial about his life and legacy:

> "Billy" Bishop did more than win seventy-two duels in the air, great and glorious as was that achievement; he gave young Canadians a feeling of kinship with aviation and the boys who read this story became the men who flew the bush planes on exploration missions to the North, dared greatly in mercy missions in storm and cold, and organized and manned the fighting fleets of Canadian aircraft which soared to hazard and fame in World War II.

I always wondered how my father had felt losing his famous father when he was just thirty-three.

Shortly after my brother's birth, when I was four, we moved to Toronto where my father first worked for another advertising company and then decided to take a year off to write his father's biography. As the story goes, shortly before he died, Billy discussed his legacy with his son and who should write his life story. Billy thought Dad should do it, and so Dad made a promise to his father that he would. It forged yet another bond between father and son that would live on well after Billy's passing.

Some of my strongest first memories of my father are from soon after we moved to Toronto: my Dad working upstairs in his den, banging away on his typewriter while my mother shushed me to keep my voice down.

It seemed like a very big deal, this book. Mom told me that Dad had approached his mother for a loan so he could write it, and to ensure that he could not only fulfill the promise he made to his father but also keep food on the table for his young family. My grandmother agreed, although my father grumbled that she had made him feel guilty about it — as if borrowing money from your family was some kind of sin. I don't know if my father ever paid that money back (but I doubt it).

I'd had little interaction with my grandmother up to that point. I vaguely remember her visiting us in Edmonton, but since then we had started visiting her in her spacious cottage in Palm Beach for a couple of weeks at Christmas. This was always such a treat because Granny Bishop, as we kids called her (the grown-ups called her "Smuggy," another of their pet names), was rather grand.

She certainly wasn't the kind of grandmother who would greet us at the door and sweep us up in her arms, peppering us with questions. Instead, we were usually met by Leffo, whose full name was Percy Lethbridge. Leffo was a London Cockney who had been Billy's valet, or what the English called in the day "a gentleman's gentleman." Leffo had a family of his own in England, a wife and two sons, yet he had followed my grandfather back to Canada in the 1930s. Then, out of this boundless sense of duty, Leffo had even agreed to stay on with my grandmother after Billy died. I am told that Leffo played surrogate father to both my dad and his sister as their parents were much too busy to rear children. Leffo had an influence on me, too, teaching me things like proper table manners and how to hold a knife and fork in the British fashion — that is, using both utensils at all times and never crossing one's fork over to the right hand.

Granny was not around for that kind of instruction. In fact, I wondered if my grandmother had ever seen the inside of a kitchen because she was also not the kind of granny who baked cookies or cooked glorious meals that you'd remember for the rest of your life. She had a cook for that, a woman named May who was as warm and inviting as Leffo.

My grandmother was definitely more upstairs than downstairs and might now be compared to actor Maggie Smith's imperious character in *Downton Abbey*. Granny was like the family dowager, a lady of the manor adopting the demeanour of an aristocrat. Every morning she had her breakfast in bed on a tray brought to her with the newspaper, and she rarely appeared in public before noon. We were given an audience with her only when she was impeccably dressed in expensive attire. I found her sense of superiority intimidating, and I could understand why my father was always on guard, thinking that she might scold him about something. On the other hand, I was fascinated by her remoteness. Without saying a word my grandmother commanded respect, inspiring you to be on your best behaviour whenever she walked into the room.

Another great thing about Florida was that Granny was a member of the fancy Coral Beach Club, where she, my parents, and their friends spent their days sunning themselves and drinking cocktails. While they enjoyed their time relaxing, I jumped in and out of the enormous swimming pool, and ate the club's special Christmas ice cream — spumoni with little chips of candy cane in it. I also remember walking along the beach, dodging blue jellyfish, while my mother and Granny posed for a newspaper photographer taking snaps of Billy Bishop's widow and her pretty daughter-in-law — the two Mrs. Bishops.

Life back in Toronto seemed quite the contrast. We were living in a middle-class neighbourhood called Leaside, in a brown brick two-storey rental — a rental because Dad was loyal to his father in every way, including taking his advice to "never buy, always rent!" Renting, Billy told him, was the wiser strategy.

"Owning property just ties you down," the old man told him. But Mom told me Dad didn't have enough money for a down payment to buy a house, and he was not going to ask his mother for money after the hard time she had already given him about the loan to write the book.

I didn't care if we owned or rented. I was a kid and I loved Leaside. It was teeming with young parents and their baby boom children. It is where I began to notice that my parents were considered a glamorous couple, attractive as they were. They entertained regularly, with parties that went on all night or took over the backyard on the weekends.

My Grandfather Billy, I am told, was considered a real character, and my father took after him in this respect. Dad seemed to need people to notice him. I remember one beautiful sunny May morning when I heard something make a sound — *ping, ping, ping* — just outside my window. Looking down toward the front of our house, I saw my father, still in his pajamas, aiming a BB gun at the ledge of his bedroom window. Dad was cursing and swearing away while shooting at pigeons, the coo-cooing of which, he screeched, was driving him crazy. Having shot at German enemy aircraft many times as a fighter pilot, my father's aim was excellent, so I don't think he was really trying to kill the pigeons, just scare them away. The neighbours were congregating around him and getting a kick out of the whole thing because everyone, including my father, was having a good laugh.

Dad was in his element, holding court, joking, and telling stories, and while I didn't always agree with his mischievous methods, I admit a part of me felt proud that people liked being around Dad. He was fun.

On the other hand, I had also begun to notice that our father had an irritable side. Even when he was home writing Grandpa Billy's biography, he would rhythmically pound away on the typewriter keys for a spell, and then erupt with foul language. "Shit, shit, shit," he'd spit out, ripping the sheet of paper from the roller, crumpling it into a ball, and throwing it on the floor in a final flourish of pent-up fury.

Downstairs, where my mother, brother, and I might be having lunch, we'd pretend to ignore it, but Mom was always tiptoeing around and I remember it made me feel anxious.

Like many fathers of his generation, mine was mostly absent from our early lives. Even when he was at home, he ate his lunch alone and went back upstairs. Around five o'clock he'd leave the house for his club, where he'd play tennis and then stick around for a few drinks before coming home. He never ate dinner with us except at Christmas, preferring a late dinner on a TV table in the living room after a few more drinks.

In fact, it was around this time that I was starting to realize that Dad's life seemed to revolve around a twenty-six-ounce bottle of amber liquid called Scotch. My father came home many nights with a bottle of Dewar's in a brown paper bag tucked under his arm. The bottle had a white label with a picture of a man in a red plaid kilt wearing a tall black furry hat — similar to those worn by the Queen's guards at Buckingham Palace.

The man on the label was young and handsome, with dark hair and a black moustache. It occurred to me that he looked just like my father, so for a while that is what I thought my father did for a living — that he went to work somewhere in downtown Toronto, took off his business suit, and put on the outfit on the label. Then I envisaged someone taking his picture, once for every bottle that he brought home, and once for every bottle the company sold to other fathers like mine around the world. That, I figured, sounded like what advertising might be all about — a full day's work, no doubt, and to me it sounded like a pretty neat job.

The first thing my dad did after he walked in the door and hung up his hat and coat was pour himself a drink from that bottle. It was a ritual that involved going to the icebox, twisting the plastic ice tray to dispense a few cubes into a glass (and usually some onto the floor), then loosely measuring out two ounces or more of the liquid into a well-worn shot glass and dumping the contents into his favourite tumbler.

After that he'd have another and another as he sat in front of the TV set. He would put off having anything to eat until he could barely hold a fork, and then my mother would dutifully bring his dinner on a tray to the TV table in front of him. My father would manage a few mouthfuls while moving his food around, some of it usually landing on the floor. Afterwards my mother cleaned up, often with remarks such as "I hate it when your father mashes the peas into the rug!"

Dad would stagger up the stairs to undress and finally fall into bed, and the next day, remarkably no worse for wear, Dad would be out the door right after breakfast — off to get his picture taken again for more bottles of Dewar's, I assumed.

At first I figured we were just like everyone else of our generation: parenting was left to the mothers, who provided kids with structure and routine, while dads went to the office. My mother got me up in the morning and prepared breakfast before sending me off to school. She took care of my younger brother, who was still a little guy and whom I called "Will-um," like the sound a frog makes. I couldn't pronounce the creamy last syllable of Will-*ee*yum, and calling him "Billy" seemed like too much of a burden, even for the third generation of Bishop men.

Mom cooked and cleaned, although as little as she could get away with. I could sense that being the perfect housewife in an era when that seemed important was not something my mother relished. However, she was a wonderful mother. She came to teacher-parent nights and my school pageants. She played board games and took us on picnics. She organized memorable birthday parties with exciting treasure hunts for all the kids. She stuffed my birthday cakes with fifty-cent pieces wrapped in wax paper (not the usual nickels and dimes that other mothers put into their kids' cakes).

Whenever I was home sick recovering from the flu or a cold, Mom would dote on me, and when I felt a little better, she would bring me a bristol board and coloured paper, glue, and scissors, telling me to get creative. It was blissful being with her, and I adored her for it.

Yet I needed my dad, too. I was the apple of my father's eye, or at least that's what everyone told me. I saw him most often early in the morning before he went off to work or upstairs to write. Dad would call me his little "Pookie Pie." But his attention was always short-lived. He would be there

My father and me outside our house in Leaside, Toronto, 1959.

for a minute and then he was gone. Oddly, I felt comforted that my famous but deceased Grandpa Billy was always around, if only in the air somewhere; whereas my father felt annoyingly remote, always slipping in and out when all I wanted was for him to notice me.

As winter approached one year, when I was about six, Mom asked Dad to take me — just me — to the Santa Claus Parade, an annual event that was sponsored by none other than the Eaton's department store and in which there would be colourful floats, bands, and, at the end of course, Santa himself with his reindeer.

I was beyond believing in Santa by this time, but it was novel that Dad would take me to the parade. Before that I had always gone with Mom. Dad agreed to it at first, and I can't tell you how excited I was; however, the night before the parade my parents had a party that was still going on when I got up in the morning. People were in their fancy dress, draped over beds and couches, drinking, smoking, and by the looks of my father and the number of empty Scotch bottles in the kitchen, he was in no shape to see Santa. I was very disappointed, but it just hardened my resolve to find other ways to get his attention.

The mind of a child works mostly on instinct. I figured that if I was very, very good, Dad would pay attention and even be proud of me. So began my life as a pleaser and classic overachiever, trying to be good at everything. At school I worked diligently to get as many As as I could, and I decided that I should also become accomplished at other things, like playing the piano, which was ridiculous because we didn't own a piano. When I tried to convince my mother that I could practise on a cardboard keyboard, she looked amused and gently told me that I was trying too hard.

I dug in my heels further when I pleaded with my mother to let me take figure-skating lessons. There was a local arena not too far from our house, and some of my classmates were signing up. I imagined myself flying across the frozen rink, doing spins and jumps, and I thought it would be wonderfully intoxicating to have everyone looking at and admiring me. However, this was around the time that Dad was writing the book, so at first my mother simply told me that we couldn't afford it. But then, miraculously, a few days later my mother announced that we were going shopping for skates and a pretty figure skating dress. I never discovered how my mother had convinced my father, but it was the kind of thing he did silently without any fanfare, and it made me feel that he must have loved me. I took those skating lessons three times a week after school and worked really hard to get my badges and take part in the local competitions. Still, it was my mother who drove me back and forth to the local arena; my father didn't think it was his job to come, and he always seemed too busy.

The same kind of thing happened when I asked for a bicycle for my seventh birthday. Once again my mother told me that Dad didn't have the money and that I would have to wait until the next year. However, the day of my birthday my mother sent me with a note (not to be read by me, she insisted) to a sports outlet store around the corner. After reading the note, the owner came out of the back with what looked like some fishing tackle and handed it to me. I looked at the package with disbelief, thinking maybe it had something to do with my birthday party, and started on my way back out the door when the man shouted — "Hey, I'm only kidding. Come on back!" He went into the back again and this time came out with a shiny new red CCM bicycle. I couldn't believe it! My dad had come through again, and this time he was waiting when I got home to help me try it out. I fell off on my first go and cut my knee. Dad simply said, "Just get back on and try it again — you can do it!" Thrilled that he had such faith in me, I did, and I made it to the end of the block. Turning around, I saw my father beaming at me.

The problem was that Dad would always disappear again, and I would be back where I started, looking for ways to attract his attention. One night my father finished his dinner and, having drunk quite a bit by that time, bumbled up the stairs to pee before bed. I'd been downstairs, too, but it was around nine o'clock, my bedtime, so I followed behind him on the way to my room. When I got to the upstairs landing, I observed him in the bathroom at the end of hallway. He'd left the door wide open, as he usually did. Standing hunched over the toilet with his back to me, I could hear him, loudly draining his body of fluid while he swayed from side to side, trying to hold himself upright.

Without any thought of the consequences, I blurted out what I thought to be a simple fact. "Dad, you're drunk." It was a word I had probably heard somewhere, but I was unsure of what it really meant.

Dad zipped himself up and turned to me with a puzzled, almost startled, look before his face and voice transformed into a storm cloud. The next thing I knew he was screaming at me: "Don't you ever, EVER, say that to me again! DO YOU HEAR ME? I don't want to hear that EVER! Now get out of here!"

I was paralyzed for a moment but then ran to my room and wept uncontrollably, as children do, as though the world was coming to an end. I realized many things about my father then; some were indelible realizations that would stay; others I would have to relearn repeatedly, cyclically, throughout my life. My father was two people: one the jokey, fun-loving, enthusiastic raconteur who could hold a roomful of guests in thrall with his stories, dervish-like; the other a potentially raging beast whose anger was always present, at a steady simmer, like a shadow just behind him, ready to leap out on a dime. And I feared I could never tell which one he would be, or what would flip the switch in him.

CHAPTER 5

WHY AREN'T WE RICH?

When I turned eight, we moved into the house where we lived until I was seventeen years old. It was right across the street from an open section of the subway where you could hear the trains come and go, *clickety clack, clickety clack* all day long, a sound which, surprisingly, you can get used to. The house was a little closer to the centre of town and in a good neighbourhood, but in terms of its overall state, it was a step down from the one in Leaside. Dad said the rent was cheap, and that seemed to be important to him.

Dad continued to work on his father's biography, but was also gearing up to strike out on his own with a public relations company he started in 1964. He called it PPS Publicity (only my father could come up with a name like pee-pee publicity), which stood for Packaged Publicity Service. His motto was "Let Us Make News for You," and he certainly was good at that. Dad had unlimited reserves of enthusiasm for finding a story in just about anything, from bug spray to mall openings, and over the years he often enlisted my little brother and me to help him. My brother, now "Bill," still bemoans the times he had to dress up as a frog or a rabbit to draw people in to some event or another.

"Years of therapy getting over that," Bill jokes, only half kidding.

Dad often brought home new products for us to test out. One Saturday morning when he was full of manic energy, he decided to try a new kitchen product that he was promoting. He proceeded to use multiple cans of the foam cleaner to clean a single pot. I think one would have done the trick, thank you very much!

"Watch how clean I can get this pot!" Dad gleefully exclaimed. Indeed, the pot was cleaner afterwards, but the rest of the kitchen was a disaster.

One of the perks of Dad's PR business was that he had a flashy car — leased, of course, which meant he got a new one every two years and always had the latest model. He was the first in our neighbourhood to get a convertible, a tan-coloured Pontiac Parisienne that I thought was just dreamy. People stopped to stare when Dad drove us around with the top down.

Our houses never quite lived up to the image Dad created with our cars. They usually had all sorts of things that needed fixing. Instead of undertaking repairs, however, my parents just painted over things to make them look shiny and new. Someone once gave Dad a couple cans of neon green paint, and he used it to refresh our shabby garage. It was a hideous colour. I was sure astronaut John Glenn could see it glowing from space as he orbited the earth. Thankfully, the garage bordered our back garden and was not visible from the street.

Our mother made valiant attempts to cover and hide flaws inside the house with her decorating skills, at which she seemed exceedingly talented. She liked to paint each of the rooms a different colour, her favourites being green, pink, and turquoise — she really loved turquoise, and painted every living room we ever had that colour.

In the end, however, it didn't make a whole lot of difference what they did. It all felt a little fake, as though we were just covering up the flaws without addressing them head on. Our house always looked frayed around the edges, lived in if not exactly worn out, as if it were being held together with Silly Putty and covered over with cocktail napkins. We had oil furnaces that sometimes ran out of oil or simply broke down in the dead of winter, pipes that groaned, a roof that leaked, and toilets that didn't always flush. And we had landlords to match — friends of Dad's who never came around to fix anything.

My mother was embarrassed, I think, because she would often tell me that when Dad's business took off, it would be different, but she didn't sound all that convinced.

None of this really mattered to my little brother and me. We were making new friends. We loved our schools, which were within walking distance. We had a couple of dogs, Fida (feminine for Fido), a beagle mutt, and McVitie (named after the English biscuits), an adorable pup that was probably a cross between a dachshund and a small hound mix of some kind.

Like we did, our dogs had the run of the neighbourhood with little or no supervision. They'd head out alone together after wolfing down their breakfasts, and sometimes Bill and I would run into them in the park.

Occasionally, we would get a call from the Humane Society telling us to come and pick them up. "Your dogs were found riding the subway again," the caller would tell us after Fida and McVitie had somehow made their way into the station at the end of the street, down the stairs, onto the platform, and into a subway car. My father thought this was a riot. He felt it underlined our family image of being a little unconventional.

This all seemed to make up for the fact that we weren't rich. I had never thought much about this or even cared until someone came over who was a friend of a friend, and taking a good look around asked me, "How come you're not rich?" assuming for two reasons that we should be:

1. because we were related to Billy Bishop (and famous people are all rich, right?); and
2. we had a grandmother who was related to the Eatons.*

I certainly felt rich at Granny Bishop's houses in Florida and in Ottawa (where she spent the summers). My grandmother was very Victorian, and she liked to do things in a British upper-crust manner. We ate large breakfasts every morning with eggs, toast with perfectly formed butterballs, the finest English marmalade, and only freshly squeezed orange juice. The table was set with starched white linens, fancy silverware, bone china dishes, and delicate Staffordshire teapots. Lunch was just as formal, and then around 4:00 p.m. it was tea time — after everyone had a nap. This was when I acquired my lifelong habit of drinking industrial-strength English tea made with hot water that had reached a rolling boil.

My grandmother's houses were also filled with memories of exciting times gone by. For instance, she had a pair of gilded chairs, one of which she told me Winston Churchill had sat in when he came for a visit. Winston and Billy had been friends, and Winston had once come to my grandparents'

---

* My father told me that my grandmother had a 50 percent discount at Eaton's on anything she wanted. The discount apparently didn't apply to subsequent generations, although my parents told me Granny allowed them to use her discount to buy furniture when they were first married.

home to discuss the possibility of Billy using his political connections to recruit Canadian and American air power during the lead up to the Second World War. I now have those chairs in my house, and I always wonder in which one the mighty Churchill sat.

Another remarkable thing about visiting my grandmother was her dollhouse. It was one of her most prized possessions and a great source of wonder among the grandchildren. You see, Granny herself had built a miniature Victorian-era house, painstakingly recreating pieces of tiny antique furniture for a living room, dining room, and master bedroom. There were hand-carved chairs, tables with wood inlay, brocade-covered sofas, a canopy bed, hand-painted portraits, and by far the most exquisite piece, a grand piano about six inches wide and four inches tall with minuscule ivory keys and strings. Some of the pieces, in fact, were replicas of the furniture that my grandmother had in her house. For a girl my age, that dollhouse was a piece of heaven.

I distinctly remember Granny sitting at her card table by the picture window making the miniatures. Every year a new intricate piece would appear — the work and time it must have taken her! As children we could sit and look at the house but, of course, we were never allowed to touch or play with it. Still, I wanted to live in that house where everything was so perfect and elegant, just like at Granny's house.

"So how come we AREN'T rich?" I finally asked my father one day. He surprised me with a ready answer, as if he had already given this considerable thought. He told me we were decidedly the poor branch of the ever-expanding Eaton family tree. We had nothing to do with the business of managing or building the national store chain that had grown (but would eventually perish) into the fabric of the Canadian identity, so that would not be a source of affluence for us.

Dad also explained that there were two things I needed to understand about wealth. First, that there were "FOOFs," which he said stood for "Fine Old Ontario Families." And then there was "FOOM" — "Fine Old Ontario Money." FOOFs usually had plenty of FOOM, he said.

"So what are we?" I asked.

"In between," Dad continued. We were technically FOOFs but without any FOOM because the FOOM that our side of the family once had was now gone.

Dad told me more about my grandfather and the war hero's erratic financial history and pattern of making money, then spending or losing it all. Billy had profited well as an author and speaker after the First World War. But then he lost the money in his failed attempt at running the small regional airline he started with fellow fighter pilot Billy Barker. He made money in England working in business, but then he lost it all in the stock market crash of 1929. Returning home to Canada, my grandfather continued to build a career in his roles with the Air Force before and during the Second World War, and he also maintained his position as a senior executive at the oil company. My grandparents lived a posh lifestyle, burning up both Billy's earnings and some of Granny's inherited resources, so by the time Billy died, there wasn't much left to pass on to us.

That's how I came to understand that money wasn't plentiful in our household. We weren't poor, but I was aware that money was an issue. And to be fair, that was only partly to do with the lack of a healthy inheritance. Dad's relationship with money was similar to his father's; although Dad never was able to make the kind of money his father had. Dad was always struggling to make money, and he must have felt the pressure to provide for his young family; but then when he had money, such as the time Dad made a quick ten thousand dollars on the stock market, like his father he spent it, in that case on an extravagant trip to Mexico with my mother.

Still, because of their family history and upbringing, both my mother and father knew a lot of rich people, many of them considered the pillars of the Canadian establishment in that era. Dad kept a membership at his exclusive tennis club, but outwardly he didn't seem to care or feel he had to keep up with the rich people who went there. He had the status and prestige of the Bishop name — a FOOF without FOOM, as he put it. And to him, there was a certain dignity in that.

Personally, I longed to be a FOOF *with* FOOM. I wanted the lifestyle that my grandparents had and that I had heard so much about. I didn't want to live in what seemed like a bit of a twilight zone — where, as a family, I believed we oscillated between feeling special and not feeling good enough.

CHAPTER 6

TOO MUCH OF A GOOD THING

With military discipline my father awoke each morning to the sound of some internal alarm and, still in his pajamas, did his exercises in the upstairs hall. Dad followed the Royal Canadian Air Force's 5BX plan, which included sit-ups, push-ups, stretches, and running on the spot. It took all of eleven minutes to complete. He did this every day without fail. Between that and playing tennis several times a week, Dad stayed in fighting form.

After his exercises, and while he shaved, he would talk with us as we made our beds and got dressed. Topics varied — something that happened the day before, something funny someone had done, or maybe another short story about his father, like the time when Dad was twelve years old and Billy took him flying. Billy took off and headed north to a local golf course, where he located four of his friends putting on one of the greens. "The old man alerted me by tapping me on the back of the head and pointing down," Dad said. "And then we dove, right at the golfers." Dad chuckled to himself as if imagining his father suddenly spying a German Albatros at six o'clock and diving after its tail.

"Weren't you scared?" I asked.

"I was, but I trusted the old man. He'd lived through a hell of a lot worse. And you should have seen the players scatter!" Dad said, his arms flaying out to illustrate.

Those morning talks were precious times to me because that was when Dad was the most upbeat. He was sober then, too. Similarly, he was at his best for a short while when the first cocktails started to flow right after he came home or when people came over. Dad put on his performing hat and he was fully "on."

"If we could just bottle your father and let him out for a few hours at cocktail hour and then put him back in the bottle afterwards, we would get the best of him," my mother joked.

Indeed. Dad thrived when he had an audience, and he appeared to get his energy from other people, which my family told me was very much like his father.

I had begun to notice as well that Dad had an addictive personality with little capacity for moderation, especially when it came to any kind of substance. Granny Bishop would say to me, "When it comes to your father, it's all or nothing. If he discovers that one pill is good for you, he will take five."

This tendency is illustrated in a particularly sad story about the time our budgie Harry started molting — seriously molting. In fact, he wouldn't stop scratching one spot and had almost plucked it clean. Mom, Will'um, and I took a trip to the pet section of Woolworths to find something for itchy birds. The checkout lady assured us that the spray we picked up would do the trick nicely.

When we got home, poor Harry was scratching ever more fervently, and as we were preparing for the first treatment, Dad came home. After the first drink was poured, he spied the spray bottle near Harry's cage. "Oh, I see you found something for Harry. Let me see."

"Arthur," our mother warned, "be careful."

Dad perused the bottle's instructions for a moment. "Okay, it says, we need to spray Harry four times every hour."

And then he was off.

Swoosh, swoosh, swoosh, swoosh.

"Look, he likes it," Dad said.

And he was right. Harry seemed to enjoy the attention and plumped up his feathers as if taking a luxurious bath.

An hour later, Dad was back to his pet project. "Here, Harry, a little more." *Swoosh. Swoosh. Swoosh. Swoosh.*

We lost track of the hours that passed where Harry was swooshed four times, and maybe one more here and there for good measure. It was, once Dad took over, out of our hands.

"Well, that should do it," our father announced, now fully lubricated and staggering from side to side.

And he was right about that. The next morning we found our beloved Harry lying at the bottom of his cage, dead as a doornail, asphyxiated probably. But at least he wasn't molting anymore.

Of course, it had all been a mistake. Taking another look at the label, we discovered Dad had completely misread it. It didn't say spray your beloved budgie four times an hour until dead, but rather spray him ONCE every FOUR HOURS!

I cried over Harry's untimely death. I blamed myself for letting it happen, but mostly I blamed my father and hoped he realized he had gone too far. It just added to my fretfulness about what he would do next. Around my father, I came to expect drama. And while I enjoyed it when it was harmless fun, I hated it when I feared it might turn into a tirade.

On Victoria Day, kids and parents in our neighbourhood in the sixties would congregate at a different neighbour's house every year for hamburgers, games, and, when it got dark, fireworks. The best part for us kids was lining up and, under the watchful guidance of the hosting father, getting a chance to set off a big one, the kind that rockets high into the air and then bursts into a beautiful pattern of colour.

Will'um and I looked forward to going every year, even though our parents never came with us. "Just not our sort of thing, darling," Mom said. That was code. I knew Dad needed to be among "his people" — those friends and admirers he already knew, who would indulge him and allow him to be the star of the show. He also wouldn't do anything that might interfere with his drinking schedule.

But I knew we couldn't avoid it forever; one day it would be the Bishop's turn to host the Victoria Day party, and I dreaded that day. I enjoyed the predictability of how things always played out at other people's houses. But I knew I couldn't control that at our house. Still, I figured it was worse not to take our turn, so I ventured to take a risk and finally invited the neighbours over to our house.

"Now, are you sure your parents have agreed to this?" one of the Ward Cleaver–like fathers asked when I made the offer. I think I was starting to feel guilty about going to the other neighbours' Victoria Day parties over the years, and perhaps I was thinking that I wanted my parents to be part of it — like a real family.

"Oh, sure," I replied.

I think I quietly mentioned to my mother that I had invited the neighbours over to our house, hoping that she would be the one to tell Dad. Except that didn't happen. If my mother did remember our conversation she certainly didn't say anything to my father. So that Victoria Day morning — a sunny, beautiful, clear day when the temperature soared to a promising 24° Celsius — I asked my parents, "So, when are we going to buy the fireworks for tonight?"

It was morning. He was sober. I was thinking, *This might work.*

"What are you talking about?" Dad peered at me over his morning newspaper.

"We are hosting the fireworks party tonight, Dad," I said excitedly. "Everyone in the neighbourhood is coming, so we need to get hamburgers and fireworks, pots to put them in."

My father's face suddenly changed from mild interest to shock. It looked as if somewhere in his head a volcano was erupting.

"WHAAAAAAT? What the hell are you talking about?"

Oh, boy.

"There is no fucking way we are having the neighbourhood over here tonight freeloading off us and drinking our booze —"

Ah, okay, so that's what he's worried about — people drinking his liquor.

At this point, I was freaking out inside but clinging to the idea that I still might be able to fix it. "Oh, Dad, you don't have to worry about that. At the other fireworks nights there isn't any drinking — well, just maybe a beer or two, but it's mostly soft drinks — and the parents are really nice and they help us kids…."

I didn't get a chance to finish.

"Diana, you just march out and tell everyone that there will be no party here tonight. Cancel it. Now!" Dad barked at me.

And for once I barked back.

"WE CAN'T!" I blurted out, thinking of the humiliation I'd feel if I had to tell everyone my parents didn't want to have the fireworks display. "I promised. We have to do it. I will do whatever you say, but we have to do this."

"Arthur," my mother said meekly, "maybe we can pull this together. These people have been awfully good to our kids…."

"No fucking way," my father yelled back. "Of all the goddamn most ridiculous schemes. Diana, go to your room."

And do what? Be eternally mad at you? That's what I was thinking, but I didn't say it. At that moment I hated my father. I hated him for making a fool of me. He could just once give in, couldn't he? I wasn't asking much, was I?

I sat down on my bed and I cried and cried. I realized I was angry about much more than just this. I was furious with him for all the ruined houses, for all the burnt up cars, for never reading my report card, for never taking me to the Santa Claus Parade, for never being there when I needed him. And I needed him. He was my father, damn it! You only get one. I wanted a good one.

I'd never let myself feel so much anger, and my wrath felt like an alien creature living inside me. My anger was a tangible thing, ready to jump out of my body at that moment and go haywire. It frightened me. Girls were not supposed to get mad. Or at least, my mother never did.

My brother poked his head in.

"Will'um," I said, trying to appear very calm now. "You have to promise me you will always hate your father. He is a bad and mean man. Promise me you will always hate him." I traumatized my poor little brother that day. He never forgot it.

But then something strange and unexpected happened. My parents didn't cancel the party. Somehow they pulled it together. The neighbours started arriving, and I could hear my parents warmly greeting them as if our earlier scene had never transpired, and in fact, they never mentioned it to me again. As I slowly made my way downstairs, I whispered to myself in my best Rod Serling voice, "You are travelling through another dimension — *do do do do…!*"

Our backyard was the royal pits compared to our neighbours'. It was long, but narrow — no more than six metres wide — with a hedge between our house and the next door neighbour's, and on the other side sat that horrific neon-green garage. Not the ideal location for a fireworks display. Still, there were hamburgers on the barbecue, and we younger folks drank Coca-Cola and played games. As it grew dark, I looked back at our lit-up screened-in porch and noticed that something was definitely different about this year. My father was animated, and people were laughing a little too loudly but appearing to be having the best time ever.

It may have had something to do with their highball glasses. The Bishops had brought a new element to the party — the hard stuff: Scotch neat and on the rocks, Bloody Marys, rum and cokes, and gin and tonics instead of the usual sodas and beer. As a result, this year our normally reserved neighbours had become a howling, reeling pack of fun-seekers. I was starting to think our party, despite everything, was going to be the hit of the season after all and that I could relax.

But then I noticed that some of the younger kids were getting really pissed off. It was getting dark and the parents had forgotten about the fireworks display, which, for us, was the whole point of the evening. When someone brought it to my father's attention, Dad staggered over to the pots, lighting off all the good ones himself.

"Hey, no fair," one kid complained. "What's your father doing? We're supposed to get to light the firecrackers!"

My brother remembered that Dad said that it was too dangerous for the kids to light off the fireworks, uttering something about liability.

I don't know what I was more upset about — that after almost not holding the fireworks party at all, my father had managed to hijack the night (considering he didn't even want it to happen in the first place); or that my father, that our family, was now exposed for everyone to see. Maybe they'd known we were different, anyway. I really don't know, but I felt then that I could no longer hide from my peers what my father was really like. Their parents all seemed to have enjoyed the evening, though, and had gone home "well lubricated."

That's when I began to realize that not all families were like ours. I had a good friend named Debbie, who lived around the corner. Her parents were right out of a fifties TV show like *Ozzie and Harriet* or *Father Knows Best*. Debbie's mother spent a great deal of time in the kitchen baking mouth-watering peanut butter and chocolate chip cookies, brownies, and Nanaimo bars (my favourite). Debbie's father was very kind and even-tempered, and he would always ask you how you were doing like he was really interested. He was handy, good at fixing stuff around the house, too, and very attentive to his children. Their household had lots of rules and structure, and it all felt a little confining, but it was different and something I knew little about.

I remember my parents went south on vacation a few times and left my brother and me in the care of a service while they were away. The women they sent us didn't always work out too well. My brother and I are pretty sure one in particular pocketed most of the money my parents left for food and supplies because there was never anything much in the fridge except doughnuts and pop. My brother and I supplemented our diet by appealing to our neighbours for an extra meal here and there. What they must have thought!

We were absolutely delighted, then, when we landed in the care of a lovely older lady, Mrs. Walker, who made us the most divine meals. A contrast to the others, for sure. But I also remember that the house was really quiet. It was nice for a change, but I wasn't used to it. It felt so empty, and it scared me, as if this were what it would feel like if my parents died.

I also recall the time when Will'um accidently hit himself on the back of the head with a baseball bat and my parents had to take him to the hospital to be treated for a concussion. I was twelve years old at the time, and Mom and Dad sent me to stay overnight with a childless couple who were frequent guests at our home. I think they saw a rare opportunity to practise some high-level child-rearing skills with me, so off I went with them to spend a day and night at their house.

Everything was so perfect, in its proper place, and never in my life had I received so much nurturing in such a short time period. I responded to this by grabbing hold like a puppy with a new chew toy. The couple helped me with my homework, brought me a cup of cocoa before bed, and then drove me to school in the morning. All new experiences for me. I felt both fostered and confounded all at the same time by this unexpected display of textbook parenting. It was like a short vacation at a spa or something. But I also clearly remember that it made me uncomfortable, and I couldn't wait to get home to what was familiar.

CHAPTER 7

THE GREAT ESCAPE

I fondly remember our home being "party central," and as I started to mature as a teenager, I began to appreciate the eclectic group of people who came through our house. Both my father and mother attracted and enjoyed the company of colourful, even eccentric, types who dropped by to have a drink. Many of them came from the creative worlds of publishing, advertising, and entertainment, and they included some of the more well-known Canadians of the day, larger-than-life characters like John Bassett Sr., who owned the *Toronto Telegram*, and Jack McClelland of publishing giant McClelland & Stewart, which had recently published *The Courage of the Early Morning*, Dad's biography about his father that had soared onto the bestseller list.

Among the other colourful personalities who visited the Bishop household was Lord Shaughnessy, a friend of my father's (they had gone to Bishop's College School together as children) whom we all called "Shag." Along with his upper-class pedigree, Shag had a rugged voice, an infectious enthusiasm, and a quick wit. Shaughnessy's grandfather had been president of the Canadian Pacific Railway and had been made a baron. Shag and my father entertained us all with verbal sparring, as if they were in some unexpressed competition with each other, a dynamic that made more sense to me when I discovered sometime later that Shag always had a thing for my mother.

Personally, I was especially thrilled when stage and TV actress Barbara Hamilton showed up at our parties. Barbara, who had acted in dozens of TV shows and stage plays, including *Anne of Green Gables* (a book that I had devoured numerous times), was the consummate Canadian actress. She was a large woman, but it was her voluminous personality that filled up a room.

Barbara's brother was the ultra handsome Bob Hamilton ("Hammy"), who had been my father's best man and a former prisoner of war. In fact, Dad's war buddies and their wives were a big part of my parents' social circle. Dad was an active member and became the director of the Canadian Fighter Pilots Association, an organization that was formed right after the Second World War for those who flew Spitfires, Typhoons, and Mustangs. There, Dad made lifelong friends who seemed bound together by hoops of emotional steel — they had the kind of loyalty to one another that comes from testing your courage together at a young age and surviving when so many others hadn't. These were guys with cool nicknames likes "Scruffy," "Ormy," "Jeep," "Hayward," and "Bish" (which is what they called Dad).

Like many survivors of the war, they didn't talk much about it when they got together, so I had little appreciation of what they had been through. They had lost many of their fellow pilots and had likely seen much destruction, but it was as if they had disassociated themselves from the trauma of war. I think there was an unwritten code among them to never talk about the bad stuff, and I didn't know then that it was something that was expected of them. These pilots had practised their lines well; so well that by their mid-to-late forties it had become a habit to remember the war as one giant party. As I heard Dad reminisce about the flying, which they all loved more than anything, the carousing with the pretty English girls ("getting laid" seemed the goal), and how much they all drank, I had to remind myself that Dad had been only eighteen when he signed up to serve in the RCAF. Being able to hold one's liquor was a serious badge of honour, almost as important as the medals they had earned and still took out to wear on Remembrance Day.

To ensure they stayed connected in their illustrious club, the fighter pilots had annual gatherings at fashionable hotels, where they brought their wives along for a nostalgic weekend of lively conversation, laughter, eating, drinking, and dancing to the music of Vera Lynn, the Andrew Sisters, Bing Crosby, and Tommy Dorsey. There were also the informal gatherings at our house on Sunday afternoons when one of the old gang would come by. On those occasions I got to be a fly on the wall, eavesdropping on their conversations and the retelling of tales about the greatest adventure of their lives.

"Best time of my life," I heard Dad say quite often, which struck me as strange. Did it mean that he preferred being shot at by the Germans to his civilian life or his life at home with us?

By this time I was starting to read more about my grandfather, too. For example, I found an old article Grandpa Billy had penned in one of my father's scrapbooks. Entitled "Chivalry in the Air," it had been published for a once-popular but now-defunct U.S. magazine called *Liberty*. "Chivalry. Of course, it existed!" began Billy's article. "Since the Wrights captured the air, there has always been a great atmosphere of romance surrounding it. The war enhanced this."

My understanding of the roles my grandfather and father played in the wars was still elementary, and I wasn't yet all that interested. But I was curious about their portrayal of war and how it anchored their lives.

"So what was it exactly that you LIKED about the war, Dad?" I asked him.

"The flying, of course."

"What else?"

"Oh, the lifestyle."

That surprised me.

"What do you mean, Dad?"

"Well, you'd go out on your mission in the morning, and when you got back [no mention of *if* you came back], you might have the luxury of a hot shower, a warm bed, and if we were lucky, a night at the mess tent or a visit to a local bar for a night of drinking and carousing."

"Sure beat the trenches!" he added.

Dad had spent a night in the dirt of the trenches but, fortunately, had done so behind Allied lines. "I couldn't sleep with all the flak," he told me, which I understood was anti-aircraft fire, where they fired from the ground skyward to shoot down enemy aircraft or keep them at bay. "I had my helmet on my head, of course, but then I thought of a better place to put it."

"Where, Dad?"

"Over my privates," he said with a smirk. "I figured they were more valuable."

That was Dad, always making a joke.

But I was back to wondering how the pilots climbed back into their cockpits after only a few hours sleep — and no doubt hung over. "How could you fly the next day?" I asked.

"We had a trick for that. We'd attach our oxygen masks, dial them up to ten thousand feet, and breathe deeeeeply. That always cleared my head," Dad said with a chuckle.

Naturally, for Dad's flying mates, Billy Bishop was the Holy Grail, and they relished hearing Dad talk about him almost as much as my father loved telling tales about him — especially the glamorous side of the celebrated war hero, the big shot.

"I remember the time the old man and I went to New York on official business when I was his ADC and we stopped in at 21 [the 21 Club was a well-known restaurant frequented by the rich and famous and a former prohibition speakeasy] for a drink and dinner. 'Billy!' people roared as we came in, as if the old man owned the place!" Dad would tell his buddies, who all nodded.

That night, in fact, Billy and Dad had dinner with Howard Hughes, the aviator and aircraft designer. "I was in awe of him, of course," my father said of Hughes, who had recently flown around the world in an aircraft of his own design.

It was the stuff movies are made of, and Dad often told the story about my grandfather's brief encounter with Hollywood. In 1942, when the Second World War was in full throttle, Billy was asked to be in a Warner Brothers movie called *Captains of the Clouds*, starring James Cagney. Cagney played a bush pilot contemplating whether to sign up to fight and deciding that he needed some inspiration from Billy Bishop, who Cagney's character described as "the greatest pilot of them all."

My grandfather, then Canada's Air Marshal, had a small but pivotal role as himself. In his one on-camera scene, while pinning wings onto a new lineup of RCAF pilots, my grandfather hears Cagney flying low overheard and shouting "Hey, Billy. Billy Bishop!" forcing my grandfather to stop what he is doing to look skyward.

Our family album has photos of the making of the movie, which was partly filmed in North Bay. But Billy also went to Hollywood to promote it, and I get chills every time I look at the picture in which my grandfather is surrounded by a bevy of Warner Brothers leading ladies. Billy appears to be staring rather lasciviously at none other than gorgeous Rita Hayworth, who is pictured to his extreme left.

Billy poses with a bevy of Hollywood beauties, including the gorgeous Rita Hayworth (second from left), on the set of *Captain of the Clouds*, 1942.

As my father tells it, actor Dennis Morgan, who was also in *Captain of the Clouds*, had encouraged Billy to approach Hayworth. "Billy asked Dennis, 'what about that Rita Hayworth?'" my father said. Dennis apparently replied, "Billy — find out for yourself. Take her down to the cabana, and #$#%$ her ass off. She loves it."

Whether this was merely bravado or something more was left to our imaginations, but Dad and his war buddies got a kick out of thinking of Billy as the ultimate playboy.

"Your grandfather was a swinger before the word had been invented," Dad said with obvious pride — as if sons of famous men all wanted their fathers to be swingers. Of course, I didn't really know what a swinger was when he said that, but I am pretty sure Dad meant that Billy was fooling around. That kind of promiscuity didn't surprise me as I had been brought up to expect that "this is what men do" and that the roles in marriage had different expectations in my grandparents' era. I also don't think he meant that Billy was a wife or partner-swapper, as the term "swinger" often means today. Still, I wondered how much my grandmother knew and how she had handled it.

"What would Granny do if she suspected Billy had his eye on someone?" I asked my father one day.

"Well, one time your grandmother actually invited two or three of Billy's paramours over to lunch," my father said.

"What? All at once?' I asked, incredulous.

"Yup, and the old man didn't know anything about it until he walked into the dining room to find them all there," Dad said.

"How did Billy react?"

"He just pretended that nothing was out of the ordinary. He was gracious and funny."

My thought on hearing this was: *what a great scene this would make in a movie.*

I wasn't sure which of his parents my father admired more in this interaction.

"But it must have been awkward?" I asked him.

"Oh, yeah, sure — but the old man got the message. Your grandmother had the money!"

*   *   *

As I said, I didn't know much about what my father or his friends actually did in the war, but I started to get more interested after I met Wally Floody, who, like my dad, had been a Spitfire pilot in the Second World War. He had been shot down in 1941 over France, was taken prisoner, and spent time in a German POW camp.

"Floody," as his pals called him, was one of the chief organizers of what became known as "The Great Escape" — the digging of three tunnels that lead to the escape of seventy-six Allied prisoners from Stalag Luft III in 1944. Tragically, all but three of the prisoners were recaptured, and Hitler ordered fifty to be executed.

Luckily, Floody had been transferred to another camp just before the escape, so he survived. He had been decorated for his role and had testified at the Nuremburg trials. Most exciting to me at the time, and really the initial reason I was interested in meeting him, was that he had also been a key adviser during the filming of *The Great Escape,* the Hollywood block-buster that featured stars like Richard Attenborough, Charles Bronson, James Garner, and, of course, heartthrob Steve McQueen.

McQueen was my movie idol and hero as a teenager. I had his poster in my bedroom, and I even named a goldfish after him. He was a so-called "Hollywood bad boy" of small but compact stature, but with an alarming smile and deep-set, penetrating blue eyes. He was cast as a rebel or a rene-gade in just about every movie he made; a real disrupter, always stirring up some kind of trouble, but often for the greater good — a character I thought must be a lot like my granddad.

When we visited Wally Floody's house, which overlooked Lake Ontario on the Scarborough Bluffs, the former POW shared with me a photo album of candid shots of the actors in the film. I am ashamed to say I was more star-struck to see Steve McQueen hamming it up with the other actors on the set than I was by the incredible feat carried out by the escape's original "tunnel king," who was sitting right next to me, but I tried not to show it.

"McQueen was a bit of jerk," Mr. Floody told me flatly, which naturally, was not what I wanted to hear.

*   *   *

Not all the people I got to meet were famous, but some stood out in other ways. For instance, among my parents' guests I remember a former nun named Mary — a spectacularly tall and beautiful woman whose story of leaving celibacy behind I never did get to hear. On the other end of the spectrum, it was not unusual for someone to point out to me that one of my parents' friends was a "nymphomaniac" (without explaining whether this was a good thing or a bad thing). Keep in mind, my parents were the type of people who thought teaching me about sex meant letting me know that there was such a thing as the "morning-after pill."

I also remember one lively cocktail party when Mom motioned to me. "See that guy over there?" she whispered. "He murdered his wife." She'd seemed quite titillated that he had come to their party, having apparently served his prison time. "A crime of passion," Mom declared, as if that made it more acceptable.

I could see that my mother loved the eccentric and quirky almost as much as my father did. She did, however, seem completely oblivious to her own beauty and how much of a draw she was at my parents' parties. Mom had movie-star looks and perfect features. She had a wide mouth, dark skin, and smoky brown eyes. She was striking like Jackie Kennedy and graceful like Grace Kelly, but she had the warmth of Mary Tyler Moore. When Mom smiled, you almost couldn't believe how perfect her teeth were. Even after thousands of dollars of orthodontic work, mine would never look that good; and so began a lifetime of feeling that I would never be as beautiful as my mother.

It was hard to feel bad about it, though, because Mom adored her children and always tried to make us feel like we were perfect in every way. Mom was without a doubt the best listener on the planet. She let you talk, and you always had her complete attention. I loved that about her, and I watched proudly as my parents' guests became smitten with my mother, the women as much as the men.

Perhaps because of our modest home and liberal ways, ours was a place where people felt they could let their hair down and be themselves, without judgment or boundaries. People smoked profusely in those days, before they knew how bad it was for them. Mom and I emptied the ashtrays almost as often as we refilled the drinks. Around that time Dad had quit smoking cold turkey after he started getting violent tremors that he called "the shakes." He was convinced that the combination of alcohol and tobacco was the culprit and dumped the latter, considering it the greater evil.

But you could certainly drink yourself silly at our house if you wanted to. It was the sixties, after all, when high-living, skirt-chasing celebrities like Dean Martin, Frank Sinatra, and Sammy Davis Jr. — Hollywood's Rat Pack — made drinking acceptable and fashionable. Hard drinking had also been the norm during the war years, I gathered. My father and his buddies drank copiously when they got together to reminisce about the times they returned from a mission alive and hit the bar "big time."

Euphemisms were used to describe "acceptable" degrees of drinking behaviour, and jokes were made about people who got *tight*, *loaded*, *hammered*, or *smashed*.

My parents both drank, but Dad was noticeably the heavier drinker of the two, polishing off multiple bottles of Scotch each week. He kept his drinking schedule to a routine that made it appear, deceptively, as though he were in control. From Monday to Thursday he worked hard, only pouring his first drink of the day after 5:00 p.m. Business people like my father generally had long "liquid lunches" out on Fridays with clients or friends, after which most did not return to the office. And on the weekends, "high noon" was high time to open the bar and to keep it open until bedtime, and by that time my dad was really "tanked."

I grew up thinking this was normal because everyone seemed to drink in those days. At that time I still didn't understand the difference between my father's drinking and that of an alcoholic — a term our family considered taboo unless used in only the most extreme cases.

"What is an alcoholic, then?" I boldly asked my mother one day.

"Aunt Jane," she replied without hesitation.

Aunt Jane was Dad's cousin on his mother's side. One single drink and she was a goner. She couldn't stop, needing another and another. Then she would turn nasty. I had been on the wrong end of her wrath once when visiting her house. One minute she was as sweet as pie (and I did adore her), the next, after disappearing somewhere for a little while, she was spewing so much venom in my direction that I didn't know what hit me. Everyone in our family knew about her "condition," such that whenever Aunt Jane came for a visit, you were advised to lock up your liquor cabinet. She just couldn't be trusted.

* * *

Rather than teaching me how to play golf or tennis, which I really would have preferred, my father instructed me how to tend bar in this environment, as if an A in "cocktail party"* would be more useful in the real world.

First rule of the bar — make sure that everyone gets a drink as soon as they arrive. Rule number two — make sure everyone always has a drink in their hand. Many of our guests drank Scotch, as my father did, so he showed me how to measure two ounces using a jigger, and add ice and a splash of water. (I took a sip of it once, gagged, and never touched it again.) Dad was also very insistent that I should never say to anyone "Can I get you ANOTHER drink?" That was considered rude. The acceptable question was simply "Can I get you a drink?" so they didn't feel anyone was keeping track, I guess. But I was. And it was *a lot*.

The drinking took on an almost carnival-like atmosphere at our cottage. The Bishops were already legendary in Muskoka, carrying on the tradition my grandfather started when he married my grandmother and became a regular guest and merrymaker at the former Eaton compound across from the stately Windermere House resort on Lake Rosseau. Because we rented (of course) our cottages and changed our location often, there was no sign with our name on it pointing the way to our place. Instead, for fun, Dad would put up a huge picture of a martini glass on the nearest hydro pole, with an arrow pointing in the direction of our rental, and that's how people found us.

Mom, Will'um, and I went up to the cottage for July and August and Dad came up on the weekends, usually with horns blazing to announce the arrival of his convoy of friends and their cases of liquor.

Over the course of the weekend the scene got louder and the merriment bolder. The atmosphere seemed highly charged and the people ever more theatrical. There might even be a drama or two: people more than a little inebriated would fall off the dock or out of a boat; a couple might have a spat in front of everyone; or someone might drive over a tree stump and get stuck, as my father did one night.

---

* This was a running joke in our family. My Aunt Jackie's children, my cousins, all say they got similar training in how to get an A in "cocktail party."

One time a group of the guys, along with my father, was playing golf at the local course. I carried the bar — three bottles: Scotch, gin, and vodka — in a rather nifty brown leather case. Every few holes, the men would stop and talk while I poured them all a short drink.

At about the eighth hole it became clear the alcohol was taking over the game when one of the more rotund players took a real whack at the ball from a tee set on a hill. He swung his club so hard that the force of it lifted him right off the ground, and he rolled out of sight. One minute he was there, and the next minute he had disappeared. It took my father and the other players a couple seconds to grasp what had happened, and then it was a half hour before they all stopped laughing.

Back home in the city, even when I was very young, maybe ten or eleven, I can remember times when my bartending took on a different spin.

Most weekends, if they were not hosting their own parties, my parents went out to friends' parties. Will'um and I would be left with a neighbourhood babysitter, and sometime in the wee hours, my parents would come home, send the babysitter away, and stumble off to bed. But not before my mother would check on us and kiss our foreheads, her perfume mixed pleasantly with the Scotch on her breath. I grew to love the subtle blending of these scents. It meant my parents were home, where at least I could keep track of what trouble they might get into.

Saturday mornings back then my brother and I would get up early and be very, very quiet — nothing made our dad so mad as to have his sleep disturbed. We'd plunk ourselves down in front of the TV to watch cartoons with our bowls of cereal and wait for our parents to stir upstairs.

When I heard the first rumblings, I couldn't wait to go and check on them. Sometimes that meant bringing them what my parents called the "hair of the dog" — an alcohol chaser to nurse their hangovers. A Bloody Mary was an acceptable morning drink at our house and usually did the trick. I poured them strong: two ounces of vodka and some tomato juice with a splash of bitters for Dad. Yep, I knew what I was doing.

Then I would bring the drinks into their bedroom where the two of them were propped up against the headboards in their twin beds (à la *The Dick Van Dyke Show*) and debriefing each other about what had gone on the night before. I enjoyed those weekend mornings in our house — my parents seemed happy and so full of fun that I couldn't wait to be an adult just like them.

As dysfunctional a routine as that seems in hindsight, sometimes my parents did something out of the ordinary that shocked me.

One New Year's Eve my parents had headed out to a party with a few drinks already under their belts, looking smashing in their party attire. Sometime in the middle of the night I awoke to hear my father arrive home, but for the first time that I could ever remember, without my mother. I heard him pay the babysitter and send her home (she lived down the street). Then Dad fell up the stairs, went into his dressing room to change into his pajamas, took a mammoth pee in the bathroom, and fell into bed.

I lay in my own bed with a creeping anxiety, breaking into a sickly sweat. *Where was my mother?* I imagined all the possible scenarios. Did Dad forget to bring Mom home? Did they have a fight? Did Mom decide that Dad was too much to handle and left us? It was as if I was reliving the terror of watching my mother being taken away on a stretcher.

I really don't know how I got through the night, and I certainly couldn't consider waking my father in his intoxicated state, so I just had to wait. Shortly after it started getting light, the front door opened and I heard my mother take off her coat and quietly go past my bedroom straight to her bed. Relieved, I plunged into a deep sleep.

I missed cartoons that morning. My parents giggling in the next room finally woke me as the sun poured into my window a few hours later. Rubbing my eyes, I wandered in to ask them if they were ready for their "morning cap." But they had already taken care of that and were sitting up in their beds holding highball glasses, sipping on drinks while they pieced together the evening before.

"So how come you didn't come home together?" I asked meekly.

Apparently, Mom had grown bored with the party, or sleepy or something, and went upstairs to take a nap.

"Without telling Dad?" I piped up.

"Well, he was busy," Mom said.

Dad looked sheepish.

"Well, what were you doing, Dad?" I asked innocently.

Dad was already chortling to himself as he began his side of the story.

"Well, there was this woman at the party," said Dad. "Guiney."

"Guiney?"

"Yep, Guiney." Short for Guinevere, he told me. "I was trying to get her pants off," he added, as if this was an everyday occurrence. My mother did not react. Then Dad continued, "The hostess caught me and kicked me out, so I took the car and drove home," he said.

"Without Mom?" I asked.

"Yeah, I guess so."

Mom's turn. She was upstairs taking a nap, remember? "And later I woke up and walked home in the rain." Mom also said she left the party but forgot her dress, apparently. She said she just put her coat over her slip and walked home.

Looking back, I think, *were my parents fooling around?* Could they have been "swingers" in the true sense of the term? They did seem very cavalier about each other's flirtations and possible dalliances. But I was never sure if any of it was true or if it was Dad just trying to make my mother jealous. While my parents laughed together a lot, I never remember seeing any overt displays of affection between them. I never saw them kiss or hug or anything. Never. Had they been more romantic when they first got married? I'm not sure. But I can say that I think Dad was the one who wanted more from my mother and not the other way around.

I only started to think about this because of something my friend Lizzie told me. Lizzie lived right next door and was only a year younger than I, which made us instant pals. She hung around our house a lot and was my guest at our cottage during the summer. One time when she was there, my parents got into their cups and started having a loud and very heated argument.

"Your father was angry about not getting enough affection from your mother or something. I didn't quite understand it," Lizzie recounted. "Anyway, the argument escalated to the yelling stage and frightened us. You, Bill, and I closeted ourselves in the bedroom upstairs to wait it out. I remember that I had to pee and you wouldn't let me."

I shook my head. I vaguely recall the argument, but there were so many of them.

Then again, something about it made sense to me, too. I always dreaded it when Dad wanted to give me a hug. It usually only happened when he was sober, so I would acquiesce but always pull away as quickly as I could from my father's grip. I didn't trust his love when one minute I was his "beautiful Pookie Pie" and the next he'd get so angry about something.

Lizzie said she recalls being there once when my father wanted a hug and I refused. "He looked livid," Lizzie said.

Anyway, the night they came home separately might explain why I felt that something was missing or had changed in my parents' relationship. It played out in various ways in their lives, but I think it might have been the one power Mom had over Dad.

CHAPTER 8

HULA HOOP QUEEN

Mom would say to me, "Your father may be a little different, difficult even, but he is never boring!" And I couldn't deny it — the man was creative. Dad was a fountain of ideas and projects, and he kept us on our toes. For one thing, I learned plenty about PR from my dad, who could get excited about selling and promoting just about anything.

At the cottage one summer he had all of us standing on the dock to cheer on his friend, Al Waits — who was no spring chicken, by the way — setting off to swim from Windermere to Port Carling on Lake Rosseau, a distance of about ten kilometres. Dad had made up posters for us to hold that said things like "Al Waits, While Others Try to Catch Up," and so on.

Another time Dad asked me to help him with a new product called PlayTape. It was an era where people played music on a hi-fi system, a piece of furniture for the living room that incorporated all your music-listening needs in one: a radio, turntable, and speakers, plus room to store vinyl records. PlayTape was the first generation of mobile music devices, about the size of a book. It had a handle that made it easy to carry around, and it played tapes on two tracks that lasted about twenty minutes.

Dad was pumped. He believed this was the next big thing. "Everybody is going to want one," he said convincingly.

Dad wanted me to test the popularity of PlayTape in a public place, and with the subway merely steps away, he suggested that might be the place to start.

Me (centre), my brother (left), and my friend Lizzie (right) posing with the revolutionary PlayTape, one of my dad's pet projects. The technology was introduced in 1966 and was an instant success.

"Lots of people coming and going. That'll be good. Make sure that you play it loud so that people can hear it," Dad instructed me.

I was afraid to go alone, so I asked Lizzie to go with me, both of us privately horrified that we would have to stand around drawing attention to ourselves in that way. All this was made more embarrassing by the fact that Dad had given us each only one tape: Herb Alpert and the Tijuana Brass —— not exactly at the top of the hit parade.

Headphones were still years away, so Lizzie and I stood at either end of the subway platform with our PlayTapes booming out "Spanish Flea" and Alpert's trumpet solo, loud enough that people could tap their feet if they so desired.

They didn't. Most stayed as far away from us as possible, and some even shouted at us to "turn that damn thing off." The plan had been to test the playing machine at each subway stop, but Lizzie and I never made it past the first one. We shut them off and high-tailed it home.

Dad turned out to be right, though. PlayTape was an almost instant success, and more than three thousand artists had published in this format by 1968. Of course, it wasn't long before more sophisticated technology came along like the Sony Walkman (with headphones!), but Dad clearly had an instinct about these things.

One of the more memorable of Dad's publicity stunts was the time when he asked me to meet him at Toronto City Hall after school one day and wouldn't tell me why. That was Dad's strategy: he knew I couldn't resist a mystery or the chance to spend time with him. Of course, I hurried down there on the subway.

When I arrived, I saw Dad and his photographer, Joe Black of Black's Photography, waiting for me with a hula hoop. *Uh oh,* I thought, *what's he up to now?*

It was 1967, Canada's Centennial Year, and the highlight of the summer was the World's Fair in Montreal. The hula hoop, originally marketed by Wham-O in the late 1950s, was past its prime popularity, but it was my father's mission to stage a comeback, and I was to be his accomplice.

"You can hula hoop, right?" Dad asked.

"A little, but I haven't done it in a while," I told him.

I am also now fourteen years old, not six.

"Doesn't matter," Dad said, forever the enthusiast. "Just take off your shoes and wade into the reflecting pool and do the best you can while we take a few pictures."

Toronto City Hall is one of the city's most distinctive landmarks, its curved twin towers surrounding a white disc-like council chamber that was modelled right out of *The Jetsons*. It is a super backdrop for taking professional photographs, especially in summer when the water fountains are gushing up in front of it.

However, my best hula hooping days were behind me, and I struggled to move my hips and keep the darn thing from falling into the water. In the meantime, a crowd had collected around the rim of the pool.

"Keep going, you're doing great!" Dad shouted as a news photographer snapped my picture and an industrious reporter took off his shoes and socks and waded over to ask me a few embarrassing questions.

"How long have you been hula hooping?"

"About ten minutes, why?" I responded with my usual honesty.

"They tell me you are planning to hula hoop to Expo, is that true?"

Oh, boy. There it was — exposed — Dad's publicity stunt to revive the hula hoop craze.

Too stunned to unmask the ruse at this point, or to anticipate the logistics of actually carrying out Dad's scheme, I told the reporter that it was news to me but that it might be fun and much better than looking for a summer job! The reporter scribbled away, and I thought to myself, *Good answer, Diana!* Wasn't I becoming a chip off the old block!

For the press, this was a good news story — what they call a "puff piece" nowadays — and the reporter wasn't about to ask any tough questions. Today, with the twenty-four-hour news cycle, someone would make sure that I trudged the 544 kilometres of TransCanada Highway between the two cities, wiggling the hula hoop as cars whizzed by. But in the sixties, a publicity stunt was just that, a stunt to get publicity. Everyone knew his role and was happy to play along. And so our family drove to Expo 67 with the hula hoop in the trunk, making the requisite stops so that I could pose for pictures in Kingston, Ottawa, and at various locations around the fairgrounds in Montreal.

The media ate it up. My picture was in all the papers and, as a result, I was branded Canada's "Hula Hoop Queen" that summer — creating quite a buzz along with a short but successful revival of the hula hoop, much to Dad and his client's delight.

* * *

In my last year of high school, when I was seventeen, we moved again, this time to a house on the edge of one of Toronto's finest neighbourhoods, Forest Hill. It sounds like a step up, but it was just another rental with the same old problems, a house in desperate need of renovations, which we ignored once again by painting over the imperfections.

My mother painted the living room turquoise and the dining room a forest green, and she decorated my bedroom in orange and pink, which you might think was rather odd, but it really worked. My room even had a fireplace, which I could not use because a lack of maintenance had made it a fire hazard. Mom moved my bed in front of it. That may have hid the big hole, but it also worried me because I feared one night as I slept, a raccoon might fall down the chimney and end up on my head.

I had reason to be concerned.

Raccoons were, and still are, the scourge of Toronto, and they regularly invaded our rooftop in the middle of the night. I think Dad felt heroic keeping his father's ceremonial sword on the floor beside his bed; he was ready to fight off these nocturnal pests.

Click clack, click clack, click clack scratched the raccoons' claws above our bedrooms.

While the rest of us might have slept through this nightly rhythm of the city, in a flash Dad would be up and out of bed, as if startled by the piercing whine of air raid sirens. He'd grab the sword and invert the handle, tassel swaying, as he used the blunt end to thump the ceiling in hopes that the din would send the raccoons scurrying.

Whomp, whomp, whomp.

"Goddamn raccoons! Fuck off!" my father snarled.

Billy's sword had no doubt seen better days. It was an authentic Wilkinson from the prestigious store in London. My grandfather had purchased it in the twenties for use on formal dress occasions.

As with Billy's medals, my brother and I loved to take a good look at the sword when Dad wasn't around. It had a hand-polished gold-plated handle and a stainless steel blade. Apparently, the blade was flexible enough that the tip could bend around to touch the handle, though we were sensible enough not to attempt that. It also had a leather scabbard with gold fittings so that it could be hung on a wall, which is where my grandfather had kept it. Well, most of the time.

Dad had also told me his father and Billy Barker had gotten sloshed one night and challenged each other to a mock duel. Even ceremonial swords have sharp tips, so both were lucky to come out of the encounter more or less unscathed. My grandfather escaped with only a slight gash to his forehead.

After my grandfather died, the sword came into my father's possession, and for a while, like Billy's other wartime artifacts, it resided in the clutter of my father's den before ending up at his bedside, where Dad had found this other use for it.

Dad had also been known to make an appearance on the front lawn waving the sword high above his head with one hand and holding up his pajama bottoms with the other (sometimes unsuccessfully) in an attempt to terrorize the raccoons, fleeing from his wrath.*

Maybe it was the war that had made him this way, but Dad was constantly on the lookout for a new enemy to fight. Sometimes this zeal had amusing and unexpected outcomes, as was the case with his vendetta against the raccoons.

Dad had decided that a good way to get rid of them might be to trap them and take them far away — far enough away that they couldn't find their way back.

"Those raccoons have sensors like a B-29 bomber," Dad claimed. (Dad had flown cover for B-29s during the war.)

So, one warm summer night, Dad filled a lobster trap that a neighbour had given him with cut-up hot dogs and left it in the backyard overnight. Sure enough, he caught one! When we all came out to look the next morning, Dad was grinning ear to ear. He decided he would drive the raccoon downtown and take him over to Toronto Island.

"Arthur, are you are out of your mind? What are you thinking? That you are going to drop the raccoon off on the morning ferry?" my mother asked.

My father thought about this for a minute and, realizing she was right, decided to drive the raccoon as far as the Royal York Hotel.

The château-like Royal York was, and still is, the grande dame of hotels in the city of Toronto. Originally built by the Canadian Pacific Railway, it faces Union Station. At one time the hotel's majestic facade was the

---

* My brother, Bill, now has Billy's sword, which he displays on a wall in his house. He has used it to mark occasions, such as cutting the cake at his wedding.

welcoming face of the city's skyline, but more recently it has been dwarfed by the construction of multiple bank towers and condominiums.

I am not sure what my father's rationale was. Perhaps he was thinking that, for a raccoon, what better way to enjoy the rest of one's life than feasting on the tasty waste of a five-star hotel? More likely he made his choice because the hotel was just a couple of blocks from Dad's office, and it would be easy to drop the raccoon off at the side entrance, which is what he did.

Unloading his cargo, Dad last saw the raccoon waddling without hesitation toward the side entrance of the hotel.

End of story, we thought, until the next day when the front page of Canada's national newspaper, the *Globe and Mail*, featured a picture of a raccoon: someone had snapped a photo of the little beast attempting to climb the brilliant gold face of the recently constructed Bank of Nova Scotia — right next to the Royal York Hotel!

It had to be Dad's raccoon, didn't it? We couldn't help ourselves; we hooted heartily over this astonishing coincidence.

CHAPTER 9

BILLY BISHOP SYNDROME

Not all of Dad's antics were a laughing matter. More than once he burnt up all the new grass in the new backyard by using three times the fertilizer that was called for. It sent Mom and me, who were sunning ourselves in the first breath of spring, scurrying into the house to escape the fumes.

Budgies might have learned to beware from the incident with Harry, but Dad also killed all the goldfish in our garden pond by putting chlorine into the water to keep it clean. When all the fish turned belly up in a matter of minutes, it was evident how much chlorine was too much.

Then he tested his new "self-cleaning" barbecue by turning it up high and dropping sheets of plastic wrap onto the grill to watch them burn up.

"See — it's self-cleaning!" Dad proclaimed.

My brother told me later that the challenge to the new barbecue made him wonder if maybe our dad was crazy. But that was just too big a word for me to take in about my father. I wanted to love him so badly that I chose to believe, like Mom, that Arthur was just different, peculiar ... and angry.

My brother bragged about it sometimes, crowing to his friends, as kids do, that they'd better be careful around us because "our dad was mean — REAL MEAN!" The thing was that he wasn't kidding. Dad's anger was no joking matter.

The worst part was never knowing what would set him off. He could be manically upbeat one minute and then suddenly, out of nowhere, ranting and raving about something. He might be drunk, but he got angry when he was sober, too, so it was difficult to stay on top of his moods.

We stood on guard, wondering which Dad we would get — the fun-loving enthusiast on some sort of intense high, or the explosive Dad who dug deep into a bottomless pit of frustration and anger.

Getting a good night's sleep was especially hard for him. If it wasn't the raccoons or the pigeons, it was street noise or our voices downstairs that would wake him up. Even during his afternoon nap, he could be roused into fits of wrath by people talking outside or somebody hammering down the street.

I can't count the number of times I heard my father rise from his bed and then bark out his window at the top of his lungs, "Shut UP and FUCK OFF!"

Dad could fly off the handle at the slightest thing, and it was always as if the sky were falling. Dad behaved as if it was the end of the world when he couldn't find the newspaper or one of his socks, when he ran out of Tums (his stomach was perpetually upset), or when he was in a hurry to get some-where — and he was always in a hurry.

Dad was an angry man, and when he drank he sometimes got angrier. Sadly, except for a few times when he directed his anger at my brother or me, our mother was his principle target, an easy one because Mom was, for the most part, his only audience at the end of day. Everything that enraged him was her fault. Dad blamed her for misplacing his keys, for burning the toast, which he did regularly, or for making him late.

There was no one less deserving of my father's verbal assault than my mother, who faithfully supported every decision he ever made — from taking time off to write a book, to renting another dilapidated house. She even worked as his assistant and administrator in the business (without pay, even!). And, of course, she was always there to make and bring his meals and clean up after him.

It pained me to hear my mother tiptoe into their bedroom at night after Dad had gone to bed, and then hear him wake up anyway with a start, growl-ing at her with language that cut through me no matter how often I heard it.

"You stupid bitch. What the fuck are you doing?" he'd snarl.

I couldn't keep track of all the things that upset him, but I will never forget the barrages. "How can you be so goddamned stupid? You useless tit!"

This was the very worst of my father, and it wasn't that my mother didn't defend herself. She wasn't afraid of him. Instead, she seemed exasperated — sometimes giving it right back to him. "Stop being such an idiot, Arthur," she'd say, but that just made him worse.

"You stupid cunt," he'd hiss and stomp off.

Language like that paralyzed me. I heard it so often, so often it made me numb and then furious. My own anger would rise up and almost overwhelm me. I wanted to lash out, scream at him, beat my fists against his chest, and tell him to stop. In those moments, I wanted to tell my father to go away and never come back. But something always stopped me. I was afraid of him, afraid that I would make things worse.

The unsettling part was that Dad was always back to normal in the morning — perky, charming, and full of funny stories, the habitual rant from the night before obliterated from his consciousness. And my mother, too, seemed to have forgotten, or at least she pretended to forget.

It was as though they'd both survived battle, and Dad's stories and banter wiped the slate clean of the fear and destruction that had transpired on their latest sortie — they were simply grateful not to be reminded of what they'd been through or all that they had survived. They had lived to fight another day. But I often wondered whether this was why my mother never hugged my father either. Was this why there was no outward display of affection between them, and why that story Lizzie told me about their argument at the cottage rang true?

Mingled with that, at least for my mother, was the hope that today might be different, a better day. I told myself, too, that maybe she was right; maybe today things would be different.

But they were always the same, and each one of us — me, my brother, and especially my mother — were absorbing the impact of Dad's unpredictable nature, each in our own way.

Slowly but surely, my brother and I bonded exclusively with our mother. It wasn't as if we made a decision to be "us against Dad." We unconsciously created a family life and routine completely separate from him.

The hour or two before he came home, we would eat dinner together and talk about our days; then Dad would arrive and polish off multiple Scotches. When he got to an inebriated state, my mother brought him his dinner on a TV table. Dad mostly moved the food around on the plate, not eating much, and then, when he was finished, he had a really annoying habit — he'd start sneezing. It only happened when he drank, and he might sneeze ten, fifteen, twenty times while blowing into a hanky before he finally got up and went to bed. That was the cue for the three of us to take over the TV room and, in hushed tones (as Dad could come flying out of the bedroom at any minute and bark at us to "shut the fuck up"), sit and enjoy a favourite program or two.

It felt to me like we were stealing these moments, and that we were betraying Dad by enjoying them without him. But the truth was, we couldn't have had such moments with him. We were just looking for some small, peaceful haven within our own home to escape to together. Leaving apparently wasn't an option.

Verbal abuse is not like physical abuse. There were no obvious external signs of its damage — no black eyes, no bruises that might call anyone's attention to our plight. Not that my mother would have sought help. She didn't want anyone to know, perhaps because most of the abuse was levelled at her.

And it may already have been familiar to her. What I knew about my mother's relationship with her parents was limited. Mom adored her father, a brilliant mild-mannered man whom we affectionately called Pa Pa Jack. He read to me as a child, and I cherished that because I knew exactly what I was getting with him and it never changed. Granny Aylen was more of an enigma to me. I was in awe of her. She had a strong personality, was super ambitious, and had developed a career at a time when women were supposed to be more concerned about getting the grocery shopping done before their husbands got home.

I'm not sure why she and my mother didn't get along. Mom said Granny was always criticizing her. I surmised that Granny might have been jealous of my mother's beauty. Granny was what people might describe as a "handsome" woman, and Pa Pa Jack was a lovely man but not known for his looks. It was a strange combination of their genes that produced my mother. And despite their many accomplishments, Mom's parents didn't seem to have great aspirations for their daughter. Mom's brother went on to become a lawyer in the family firm, but my mother said that her father thought that she should become a movie star.

On one visit to see my grandparents when I was eleven, Granny had made Mom cry about something at the dinner table. I wish I could recollect what Granny had said to upset her, but my reaction was swift. "Don't you talk to my mother like that," I bellowed. Then I got up from the table, grabbed my mother's hand, and announced, "We are going out!" And with that, my mother and I walked along Dow's Lake on the Rideau Canal for an hour together, talking and giggling about anything other than what had just happened. When we returned to the house, nobody said a word, and it was as if nothing had happened.

When I asked if we could just go and live with her parents to escape my father's ire, the look of shame that came over my mother's face broke my heart. "No," she replied, "this must remain our little secret."

Yet it didn't seem so little to me. Shame. The shame of not being who we wanted people to think we were held us together as we suffered in silence.

What I didn't know at the time was that my Aunt Jackie, my father's sister, had developed similar drinking issues. Fortunately, she was happily married to my Uncle Raymond (nicknamed "Hippo," as he had been overweight as a child), and they had three children, the eldest Michael, then Maggie, and then Catherine (nicknamed "Twink" because she was small and cute). Twink says that her parents were also in their element holding big parties that lasted until the wee hours of the morning. "Everyone would gather around the piano singing war songs, saluting all their friends who had not made it home," she recalls.

Being the youngest, Twink also remembers her mother's escalating drinking and anger. "I loved my father. I served my mother," she recollects. "In her eyes, I could do nothing right. I sometimes think she enjoyed watching me suffer. Perhaps it is because she suffered? Not sure. But I took solace in caring for my father."

I didn't know about any of this until much later. My brother and I saw very little of our cousins growing up. To make matters more complicated, my father had created a vitriolic feud with his sister. None of us was sure what it was about, but it all seemed to circle back to Billy one way or the other, and sibling rivalry over their famous father's affections.

We had such a small family, and I felt isolated and conflicted — as if I would be betraying my father if I spent too much time with my cousins.

At one point, Twink says her family decided that they didn't want my father coming around anymore, because Dad would drink too much and inevitably explode and start a fight.

"Was Billy like this? Did he drink, too?" I asked my mother one day.

"They all did, dear," she said. It was the times, the wars, she told me, and well, it was clear that hard drinking ran on both sides of my father's family. Mom was loath to use the "A" word because it was verboten in our family to call anyone an alcoholic unless, as with Dad's cousin Jane, when they took one drink, they simply lost control and couldn't stop. To my parents there was a big difference between drinking a lot and being an alcoholic.

I learned that, like Dad, Grandpa Billy's sleep was often disturbed at night, so Lethbridge put a glass of Scotch in the drawer beside his bed in case Billy needed the sleeping aid during the night.

"But did he get angry?" I asked with some trepidation. Billy was my centre of gravity, and I counted on all the stuff I knew about him not to change. I needed to feel that something in my life would always be what I knew it to be.

To my huge relief, my mother said firmly, "Never. Your grandfather may have done his share of carousing, but he never got angry. I never heard him raise his voice. He was always a gentleman."

So what had made my father and my aunt so angry? My father was taking out his anger on my mother, but was he really angry about something else? His childhood, when he'd been both spoiled and neglected by his parents? The war? The alcohol abuse? Or was it the simple fact that Dad had played a secondary role to his famous father?

Could Dad really be suffering from what my brother and I felt certain was the most dreaded of all diseases — what we dubbed "Billy Bishop syndrome"?

We had coined the term in jest. One was afflicted with Billy Bishop syndrome, we reasoned, when feeling the pressure of that larger-than-life image of a famous relative, the one everyone was always talking about with admiration — how he didn't have any faults or, if he did, how they were endearing signs of character. That relative had set the bar so high that anyone coming after him had the task of trying to live up to an impossible reflection. It meant you couldn't just be good, you had to be great! And the thing is, you really wanted to be great. Yes, if you had Billy Bishop syndrome, you craved the feeling of greatness and needed to be special, and you had a morbid fear of not standing out, of not accomplishing big or great things, of being — perish the thought — ordinary! We Bishops were not allowed to be ordinary or average. No, sir.

I definitely had the early stages of BBS — especially at school. I discovered that throwing myself into my school work helped me escape the turmoil at home, and I loved learning. But the fear of being average drove me compulsively to find ways to get noticed and stand out — such as needing to be first in my class. I became obsessive about my study habits, often going over facts and figures for hours and hours. When I didn't perform as well as I expected, or when I wasn't the best at something, I was desperately hard on myself.

I was terribly proud to have been "accelerated" — doing grades three and four together in one year, something that was popular in the sixties. But when my reading scores fell behind in grades five and six, I was inconsolable, often bursting into tears in class.

My beloved grade-five teacher, Paul Rowney, would take me into the hall and kindly ask, "What's the matter, Diana?" But I didn't really know. The humiliation just drove me harder. The payoff came the following year, when I received the Merit Badge, the top scholastic award for the whole school, which was gratifying but only served to reinforce the all-consuming cycle.

Dad, we figured, must have had Billy Bishop syndrome worse than anybody. Like sons and daughters of other famous celebrities, no matter what he did, Dad was always being compared to his father — and Dad, more than anything else, wanted to be a "chip off the old block."

If Billy was known for his antics, mostly harmless and funny, Dad tried to up the ante. Good attention, bad attention, it was all the same for Dad, as long as he was getting some.

He was like a big kid who had never been taught strong boundaries. He enjoyed finding ways to be bad and inappropriate, and there were so many occasions when he really thought it was funny to be downright embarrassing. More than once Dad answered the telephone to find someone speaking a foreign language. In those days, it was usually an Italian speaker who'd had the misfortune to dial the wrong number. While we couldn't hear the voice on the other end of the line, Dad waited a few seconds before announcing to the caller that "no wops" lived at this address.

Dad growled into the mouthpiece "We are WASPs — get it? WHITE ANGLO SAXON PROTESTANTS!" And then he hung up, chortling to himself and looking to see if we had been listening in.

"Oh, Arthur, really!" my mother would exclaim.

Another time we had been invited to dinner at an exclusive club. Dad had a weird habit of taking a bite of something and beginning to talk as he chewed. Inevitably he would start choking and coughing. On this occasion, in front of an entire table of well-heeled guests, Dad took a bite of his steak, and while gesticulating enthusiastically as he talked, he suddenly coughed up the large piece of meat right into the middle of the table. I wanted to die.

I know there were people who disapproved of my father. A friend at the cottage once told me that her mother didn't want her father hanging around with "that Arthur Bishop." As her mother told her, "He drinks too much and is a bad influence."

Still, my father had just as many fans. In small doses he could be incredibly entertaining. We loved that about him, because I think he tapped into something in people. He could be outrageous for them so that they didn't have to be or so that they could be, too. Not everyone was comfortable with that, of course, but Dad had a wide circle of admirers who enjoyed and encouraged that side of him.

Few people guessed how trying dealing with the real Arthur could be for us, his family. By this point I was becoming a young woman and feeling the weight of my family's dysfunction on my shoulders. As a result, I was driven, not just at school but at home, not to let anything bad happen to my mother, my brother, or to Dad. I needed everyone to be okay, and I wanted to make them all better. Little by little I was becoming the family fixer, feeling that I could have some peace only if I could control the chaos and make everyone around me content. It may have started with the parties — making sure that everyone had a drink in hand. Or becoming my mother's defender with her mother and my father. Or managing Dad's tantrums by jumping to attention and running around trying to solve his problem whenever he couldn't find something. That's what I had started to do. I knew if I could just find what he was looking for that it would make him stop. That would fix things for a while. And of course it did — until the next time. But I would always be on guard, waiting for the next time.

CHAPTER 10

PROTECTOR AND DEFENDER

I knew that I wanted to go to university, and it was not lost on me that this was a privilege my generation had gained thanks to our parents, many of whom never got that chance. At the same age I was trying to decide what courses I might take to further my education, thirty years earlier my father had been taking his first solo flight, anticipating flying Spitfires into combat over France.

Nonetheless, I was also feeling what perhaps Dad had experienced back then: the thrill of being on my own for the first time. Bittersweet, however, was the guilt I felt about leaving my mother. She seemed so vulnerable, and both my brother and I instinctively felt the need to protect her. Yet even Dad's anger was predictable. He was a bully and consistently verbally abusive. It didn't escalate, just stayed the same. We all expected it even if we never got used to it, so I decided I could still go away to school as long as I wasn't too far away.

I was accepted at three universities, including the University of Toronto, which would have kept me at home. I made the decision to take a liberal arts degree at the University of Guelph, which was better known for its agricultural studies. My choice was based on three things: I didn't want to stay at home; Guelph was a mere forty minutes west of Toronto; and my boyfriend had decided to go there. Since meeting at high school in grade twelve, Donnie Robinson (my first love) and I had become inseparable.

According to my girlfriend Shardie, whom I also met in high school (and who, like Lizzie, became a lifelong friend), "Donnie and Diana" were considered one of the "it" couples at our school.

"Donnie was like a hero to all of us, and the two of you seemed to be so in love," Shardie said.

I certainly was. To be frank, high school was not my finest hour. I was gawky and awkward, as teenagers can be. I was obsessed, as always, with doing well, studying, and working on my grades, the pleaser hard at work. But I wasn't a cheerleader. I didn't play team sports. I didn't know anyone on the basketball team or go to cheer at the football games.

My extracurricular activities centred mostly around music. Our school had a phenomenal music program, and I had taken up the viola. Playing in our school's various full, string, and chamber orchestras kept me pretty busy. Any free time I had was spent hanging out with my girlfriends or poring over the latest *Seventeen* magazine. I was feeling pretty invisible, definitely ordinary, until I met Donnie.

Donnie had transferred in grade twelve from a boys' private school to our public school. He dressed like a frat boy with cotton button-down shirts and chinos that he admitted to me he ironed to perfection (along with his underwear!). Donnie had big green eyes and a thick mane of straight auburn hair that he frequently flicked out of his eyes for effect. He had a swagger about him, and he was a dead ringer for actor Kevin Bacon in the movie *Footloose*. Donnie was instantly welcomed at the popular students' table at the front of the cafeteria, where the beautiful, confident girls and guys hung out at lunch. So I was floored when one day those green eyes were fixed on me at a table much farther away.

For weeks I was the object of Donnie's stares and smiles until he did something he figured was more daring: he put a note in my locker that read "Can you guess who?" Just when both of us had almost given up on finding an appropriate way to actually meet, a friend of Donnie's introduced us — a set-up — but it worked and I never looked back. From that day forward, Donnie was all there was.

My parents loved Donnie almost as much as I did; he was handsome, smart, and came from what Granny Bishop referred to as "good stock." He was related to the Phelan family, who had founded Cara Operations Limited, a food catering business for passenger air and rail travel.

Being with Donnie gave me new sense of confidence. He introduced me to coffee — we could talk for hours over a single cup — rock music (and my passion for the Moody Blues), and romance. Donnie adored picnics with

French bread, cheese, and even wine when we could convince someone to buy it for us. We drank cheap and horrible Mateus and loved it. I delighted in being a little bit naughty with Donnie: getting caught necking in the school-yard, dancing naked in the woods, and building bonfires, which were strictly forbidden on Toronto Island, a short ferry ride from downtown Toronto. Once we even missed the last ferry, and I secretly hoped we could stay there all night; unfortunately, the Toronto Harbour Police had other ideas and zipped us back across the lake with a stern warning to catch the subway home.

Donnie was a young man who commanded attention. He had presence. When he walked into a room, it was clear who would take charge. Like my father, and what I knew about my grandfather, Donnie was also completely at home being the centre of attention. He belonged there, and when I was with him, people noticed me. I liked that and so I was hopelessly smitten.

Donnie was going to Guelph because it offered a renowned program in Hotel and Food Administration (and in fact, Donnie would one day become president of the family business). He never pressured me to go to the same school. That was my decision, one I made without much reflection; but my mother, always gentle in her criticism of me, was less than enthusiastic when I told her I was following Donnie to university — not because of Donnie, but because she worried that I might lose myself in the process. "Are you sure you really want to go to Guelph?" Mom asked me, instead of asking the question I know she really wanted to ask — whether I was putting someone else's ambitions ahead of my own.

Nonetheless, Guelph turned out to be fun and exciting, and it led to, of all things, a four-year specialization in French (I had always wanted to speak French like our charismatic prime minister, Pierre Elliot Trudeau). I was awarded one of only two fellowships to do my third year at the University of Sherbrooke, a French university in Quebec.

It cost more to go away to school, of course, but I was determined. I had started taking on summer jobs when I was fourteen years old. Like his father had done for him, Dad usually found them for me, and I admit that back then I was not entirely grateful for his efforts. One of his clients owned a string of restaurants and snack bars, so I was put to work selling hot dogs at concession stands on Toronto Island and at the Canadian National Exhibition (CNE), the city's large annual end-of-summer fair, sweat pouring off me day after day in the broiling heat. It was gruelling, and I made ninety cents an hour, a pittance even in those days, but I learned the value of hard work and hard-earned money. It helped to pay my tuition plus room and board. Even so, I usually had to ask Dad to supplement what I couldn't raise myself. I knew it was hard on him, as he was just making ends meet, but this was where Dad could be wonderful. He always came through, and I didn't appreciate it as much as I should have at the time.

During the winter semester of my third year in Sherbrooke, where I was living and studying in French, I asked my father for an extra twenty-five dollars a week to get me through to the end of the term. I fully expected him to say no. Instead Dad sent me the first cheque in a card that purposely mangled a mixture of French and English to make his point — "*Ma chère* Pookie — Do NOT forget that $25 equals '*une bouteille de Scotch pour ton Pear* [sic].'"

I could see him smiling as he wrote that and it made me chuckle aloud. Sometimes it was just hard to be mad at him.

During the next four years, I came home as often as I could, either from Guelph or Sherbrooke, and found that things had remained pretty much the same. Dad was still a raging tornado, but Mom no longer put up a fight, her will calcifying into bland resignation. And she seemed sadder. My mother never intentionally projected her life onto mine, but it happened anyway. We were so close, best friends as she had predicted, and she confided in me.

"Why does your father have to always talk about himself? Why doesn't he care about what other people are doing?" These were the kinds of questions she asked me, but never the obvious one — why he drank so much.

My mother told me that Dad seemed to treat her better when I wasn't around. I don't think she meant to be unkind because she had no idea why this was true — if indeed it was — so as with most of my feelings, I just buried the confusion that comment caused for me.

With the perspective of someone living on the outside of our little family drama now, I saw my mother as someone who had given up who she was in order to make someone else happy, and no matter what she did, it would never be enough. It hardened my resolve to never let that happen to me. And in fact, while my relationship with Donnie survived the first few years of university, the year I went to Sherbrooke, I had to leave him behind and I knew it was the right thing to do whether the relationship carried on or not.

My mother continued to work for my father in his PR business, which meant they were together in the office as well at home. Fortunately, Mom was a shrewd businesswoman who kept the office on track and really enjoyed going downtown every day. But even there, Mom did not escape Dad's temper. On visits to the office and during summers when I helped out, I often caught Dad exploding over the slightest thing — an appointment change or a printing mistake. More often than not his rants were misdirected at my mother. For instance, once Dad discovered that the printer down the street had made an unfortunate mistake in the spelling of a client's name. The boxes of brochures arrived at the office and the client's last name on all of the materials was "Shitlitz."

"Shitlitz!!!" my father boomed. "It's not Shitlitz, for Christ's sake. Who would have a name like Shitlitz?" he'd seethed at Mom, whom he assumed was at fault.

Passively Mom sent the boxes back to the printer.

As it turned out, the client's name really was Shitlitz. We all laughed about it, but there was no apology from my father, and it wounded me to see him treat my mother that way. It offended me even more to see what it was doing to her.

My mother's life was getting smaller. She got up every morning almost mechanically, went to work, came home, and had a few drinks with Dad to keep him company because, as she said, "What else I am supposed to do?" She'd wait for him to have his dinner and clean up after him, and when he had gone to bed, she had an hour or two of quiet time to herself.

She would have preferred to go out to a movie or the theatre once in a while, but Mom said that everything they did had to be Dad's idea, and he certainly wasn't about to do anything that would interfere with his drinking schedule. They had travelled a few times over the years, once on that trip to Mexico and another trip to England, but those getaways became less frequent, as my mother said she didn't want to sit around watching Dad drink solidly for a week.

Not surprisingly, I felt the burden of my mother's life unlived. It cast my brother and me as protector and defender of our mother.

My brother was in his teens and still living at home while I was away at university. Because he was older now, he liked to be called Bill — no longer Will'um, and definitely not Billy, as he thought being identified with his grandfather was too much. Bill is as sensitive a guy as you will ever meet, and he was dismayed to come home some nights to find Mom crying. Listening and comforting her became his new role, but his frustration was also rising.

One night, Bill told me Mom was such a mess that he had gone up to Dad's room, woken him up from his drunken stupor, and screamed at him.

Asked if he thought it had done any good, Bill replied that he didn't think so, and the next morning Dad never mentioned it.

I admired my brother for having the courage to do such a thing. Sure, I had talked back to Dad in the heat of the moment when he was yelling at Mom, but my actions were in small rapid bursts that got sucked into the vortex of his furor and landed nowhere. The idea of confronting Dad in a calmer moment terrified me. I was afraid that if I did, he would turn on me, too, and that I might lose his love. I couldn't risk it.

The person whom I confided in most at this time was Shardie. She'd played second violin in the orchestra at high school, so we had seen and knew of each other, but I felt a kindred bond with her even before I met her — the strangest feeling, as though she had been my sister or even my twin in a previous life. People told each of us separately that we should meet because we were so much alike, with a similar energy and mannerisms, but the reason we finally met was because of Donnie. He approached me at my locker one day and said, "That girl, that one who is so much like you, well she's down the hall at her locker and she's crying. Why don't you go and see her?"

Without hesitation, I went and found her and asked if she was okay. It was as though we'd always been friends. Through her tears, Shardie said, "I got a really low mark in math and almost failed the exam."

"That's interesting," I said, "because I almost failed my English exam," and then we both laughed; neither of us had ever almost failed anything before, and at the time math was actually my best subject and English was hers. And that was it. We became best friends.

Our instant affinity was likely somewhat rooted in our similar family stories. Her mother was the one with the drinking problem, displaying manic moods and rages. Her drinking became so severe that she died from related causes at the age of fifty-four, when Shardie was in her first year of university. Long before that, however, Shardie's father had left her mother because of the drinking, and Shardie, only about eight or nine years old at the time, went to live with him.

I remember Shardie's dad as a tall, handsome, and exceedingly kind man who loved to sing. He taught Shardie and me to harmonize some old wartime songs while we did the dishes: "Oh, I get the blues when it rains, blues I can't lose when it rains...."

But Shardie's father had been a POW who also never talked about the dark side of his war experiences. However, one leftover from the war Shardie recalled was that her father was obsessed with everyone cleaning their plates. "Mom was out cold drunk one morning, and for breakfast Dad presented me with a cold plate of macaroni and cheese liberally laced with ketchup. I balked, naturally. But Dad said I was lucky to have anything at all because, as a prisoner of war, all he got to eat were potato peelings. So he just sat there while I painstakingly ate each noodle one by one, gagging on every bite."

Shardie missed school that morning because it took her until noon to complete the task. This story was so discordant with the jovial man that I knew as her father, but like my dad, Shardie's father was a war veteran with a suppressed emotional history.

My parents adored Shardie like another daughter. Likewise, Shardie adopted them as a second set of parents, and she spent loads of time at our house. "I loved your father. He was funny, quirky, and kind of adorable. I never saw your father get mad at your mother, but I do remember he had a weird pattern," Shardie said. "He would hold court in the living room," she continued. "He'd be knocking back those double Scotches, being very entertaining and social, and then suddenly, he would reach a point where he became completely anti-social, not talking to us anymore and kind of in his own world. I recognized, of course, that your dad was blasted because I'd lived through it with my mother."

I knew the pattern well. That was the cue for my mother to bring Dad his TV dinner, when we would leave him, retreating to the kitchen to eat with Mom.

"Your father would then mutely eat a little, and after that he was gone," Shardie said. "I thought it was odd that he didn't eat with your mother, or us, and that our night wouldn't really start until he had gone to bed."

I am sure some of my other friends, including my boyfriend Donnie, noticed these irregularities in our household, too, but no one ever said anything to me about them.

Sadly, Donnie and I broke up after my year away in Sherbrooke, finding the distance too wide to sustain the relationship. Donnie had moved on and found someone else. I was heartbroken, but I threw myself into my school work. Fortunately, after my last year of university, I was one of two students selected from the University of Guelph for a fellowship to go to France and teach English in a French high school in Grenoble. It was an incredible opportunity, my chance to improve my French and also to see Europe, and the best antidote I could imagine to get on with my life.

Granny Bishop chided me for letting Donnie get away. "You should have married that boy. He is a fine young man from a good family," she said. She wouldn't listen when I told her that Donnie was the one who broke up with me. "Nonsense," she said. "The woman always chooses."

And Granny may have had a point. As a young girl and now a woman, I dreamed of finding my Prince Charming, but I never saw myself marrying him. My parents' marriage instilled in me a ferocious, all-consuming independence. And not just that, but I was deeply influenced by both my mother and my two exceptionally capable grandmothers, who I felt had talents that were held back to a greater degree than their husbands. That weighed heavily upon me, and as a result, I had already started to develop a fear of succumbing to a similar entrapment.

I sensed Donnie wanted a partner who would be able to follow him around as he pursued his big career. And that was not going to be me. I wanted my own big career. I was proud of the fact that I was part of a new generation of modern women, wanting to be self-reliant and not trust my fate to anyone but myself.

My mother was thrilled for me that I was flying off to Europe to pursue my dreams, perhaps living vicariously through me, while also dreading my departure — another year where I would be away, really far away this time, and still years before the easy and cost-effective ways to communicate with smartphones, text, email, or Skype. I knew that my mother would be feeling more alone than ever, and I tried not to think that I was deserting her, leaving her with no means of escape.

That year in France was magical. I fell in love with the country, the language, and the food and wine, as everyone does, but most of all I fell in love with my new sense of freedom. In a place where no one knew my family history, there was nothing to live up to, no secrets to keep or shame to worry about. It seemed more profound an experience than being really on my own for the first time. I discovered that I was completely comfortable parachuting into a new place where I knew no one. I was rarely homesick. Deep within myself I had discovered the heart of a gypsy who derived strength from continually moving around.

I never called or connected with my parents once that whole year. In fact, my strongest tie to my family during that time was with my Granny Bishop, who, in her seventies, had gone to live in Bermuda full-time. Coincidentally, there was a long postal strike going on in Canada, so I couldn't even write to my parents. Instead, I sent missives about my life in France to Granny. I would share stories with her about the young students I was teaching, the fact that they served wine in the school cafeteria at lunchtime, about sitting in cafés sipping Cinzano, and my sightseeing adventures to the Riviera, while I was packing on the pounds eating a baguette every day.

"You don't want to get fat!" my grandmother chastised in her dispatches to me, taking on more of a parental role than I ever got at home. But I could tell that she loved my letters and postcards, and we bonded over the experience — Granny perhaps reliving her twenties (in the twenties) when she and Billy, then residing in London, often visited the Continent to attend the races at Le Touquet or to visit the French Riviera. Granny's memories of France as part of "The Lost Generation" — those who had come of age during the First World War — included stirring memories of sipping wine with Hemingway in Paris cafés and eating lunch with Scott and Zelda Fitzgerald in Nice; meanwhile, I was travelling around with a bright yellow backpack eating croissants and Mars bars for breakfast.

When it came time to come home, I found that my mother had survived my year away; although she seemed more worn out than ever. I had a choice to make. I was twenty-three years old, and I dreamed of renting an apartment of my own. Instead, I convinced myself that I needed to save some money, so I moved back in with my parents.

My father had connections at American Airlines, which had opened an office in Toronto, and he stepped in once again to get me a position as a reservations agent, history repeating itself, as he arranged work for me as his father had done for him. I was frankly delighted because when Dad did these kinds of things, I felt he was giving me love the best way he knew how. I didn't know what I really wanted to do with my life, and I was seduced by travel, plus there was some symmetry to the opportunity — Billy Bishop's granddaughter working for an airline! Within two years I had been promoted to a junior management position.

My mother was cheered by my presence, but it only sharpened for me her lonely routine. There were the cocktail parties my parents hosted once in a while, where they seemed to liberate their younger selves, but most of the time Dad came home, got drunk, and went to bed. I tried to make it up to my mother by being around more and giving her someone to confide in. We did a lot of the mother-daughter things that we loved. We went shopping and to the movies; we'd get up at the crack of dawn on a Saturday morning to go to the market; we explored new places to have lunch. We even began the practice of taking trips together on my free passes with the airline to places like New York and Puerto Rico. It felt good to whisk my mother away somewhere. On those getaways, I'd watch the colour come back to her face a little bit more every day. It gave me a sense of control over my mother's happiness, and perhaps also my own.

CHAPTER 11

CHRONIC FATIGUE

After I had been working at the airline for a few years, I started to feel unwell. It began with a simple cold. Then I got the flu, and the symptoms lingered. I'd take a few days off, then go back to work; a few days later I would be back at home in bed, sleeping around the clock. The pattern grew more intense, and my absences from work longer, until I finally felt I had no choice but to surrender to it. I was guilt-ridden about not being able to give my all, and I decided that the best thing to do was to quit my job.

I conscientiously went to my family doctor a dozen times to find out what was wrong with me. I was terrified that it might be serious, but mystified that no one knew what to make of it.

My mother was obviously very worried, but a great support. I don't know what I would have done without her, telling me every day that I would get better and that much more interesting times were ahead for me.

My father, on the other hand, had never been good with people around him getting ill. When my mother got sick, which was fortunately infrequent, he tended to ignore her until she got better. It was as if he could not handle anyone or anything taking the spotlight from him. I felt we were letting him down if we couldn't function as we normally did. So with this new mysterious development in my health, Dad was evasive. He privately told my mother that he didn't think there was anything wrong with me. He said I was probably just reeling after getting rid of a "deadbeat boyfriend" I had been seeing for a couple of years. Dad had been right about that guy, but I was the one who had broken it off, and it wasn't until months later that I had become sick. That didn't seem to impress my father, and I was hurt. Did he think I was faking it? Did I? Was I crazy and making the whole thing up? Why would I do that?

I tried to keep things light with Dad, even joking that my doctor probably wasn't a real doctor at all, as he didn't have any answers. I started calling him "Mr. Blank." My father thought this was very funny.

"Are you going to Mr. Blank again?" he would ask, avoiding any direct discussion of the situation.

"You mean Mr. Blank, who pretends to be a doctor?"

My father howled. I loved it when I could make him laugh.

"Yeah," I said, "I am going to see him again today, but it won't do any good."

And I was right. Mr. Blank would simply write a few notes and tell me to go back to bed until I felt better. But no matter what I did, I didn't feel better, and, in fact, I was getting worse — the fatigue I was experiencing was debilitating to the point that I slept fourteen hours a day, getting up to have breakfast, seeing my parents off to work, and then going back to bed. I would wake up to make myself a sandwich and read a little bit around noon, but I was so zonked by even that little effort that I would sleep again until my mother came home around 6:00 p.m. Mom, Bill, and I would have dinner together, and then we would wait until Dad was in bed and out of the way before we would talk and maybe watch TV. The same routine repeated itself day after day, but no matter how long I slept, I wasn't getting any better.

I still cannot believe how patient my mother was, and it made me feel horrible that I was worrying her so. She was horrified that, while I was in the prime of my life, I couldn't walk up a flight of stairs without becoming seriously out of breath and having to lie down. She believed I was sick. She just couldn't do anything to help me. I felt I was just adding to her burden.

It never occurred to me that, in addition to what was physically going on with me, I might actually be suffering from some sort of undiagnosed depression. I was, after all, a grown woman living at home with her parents under disheartening circumstances. But as with alcoholism, people didn't talk about depression in those days, especially in a twenty-something who had been such an overachiever. I remember being incredibly frustrated but not having the energy to dwell on it.

There were certainly days when I was despondent. My friends had long since stopped asking me how I was. Few even came to visit anymore. Shardie had married and moved out west, or I know she would have been there to console me. I tried not to think too much about her life or of my other friends who were moving on, finding partners, getting married, and having children. More troubling to me was the creeping realization that I didn't want these things for myself, and I wondered why not, and why I felt so stuck.

When I allowed myself to dream, I pictured a great career with lots of adventures — a life unleashed, without responsibilities to anyone or anything, as I had in France. But that dream seemed unattainable, at least for the moment. I would start to feel just a little better, so I'd stay up an extra hour one night only to find that I'd relapsed the next day and had set myself back weeks. It was terrifying. I felt trapped in a recurring nightmare with no escape. I was so tired I didn't recognize myself anymore. *Who is this person?* I kept thinking. *It's not me.* Sleep was all I wanted.

It was my grandmother who provided the first lifeline to my recovery, albeit a long, slow one. Granny Bishop invited me to convalesce (as they might have done at a sanatorium in her day) in Bermuda, where she now lived with her new husband.

Out of respect for my grandfather Billy's memory, my grandmother had waited until the fiftieth anniversary of their 1917 wedding before she married again, this time to a very different sort of man — thoughtful, attentive, and conservative, a notably sharp contrast to the effervescent, buoyant, impulsive Billy Bishop.

I remember her wedding well. I was fourteen and my grandmother was in her early seventies. She had met Hugh Hughson, also widowed, in Ottawa. They married in the little chapel at Timothy Eaton Memorial, where fifty years earlier my grandmother had walked down the aisle with Billy in the larger main section of the church.

Both families attended, delighted to see romance blossom again for these two senior citizens. At one point a small plane circled overhead and the chapel went quiet for a moment as we all started to whisper. "It's Billy," someone piped up as spontaneous laughter broke out from all of us.

The newlyweds took up residence in Bermuda, where Hugh purchased a home, and I had visited them periodically since my trip to France while I was at American Airlines. We had become closer, but still I was surprised when Granny offered to pay for my ticket and insisted I keep it open-ended. She wanted me to stay until I got better.

Going there always felt like such an indulgence, even then, when I was not feeling my best. It took all the strength I could muster to take the three-hour flight to the small island in the Atlantic, and when I arrived at their home in Paget, I immediately headed into the kitchen to the welcoming arms of Edith, Granny's Bermudian maid and cook (May had retired), before wending my way into my grandmother's back bedroom. There I found Granny propped up in bed. She'd had some good years here in her new home, but now she was dealing with the debilitating effects of emphysema, the consequence of a lifetime of smoking. It left her short of breath and sometimes gasping for air.

"Don't ever start smoking, Diana," Granny cautioned me sternly as she sputtered and choked. "Or you will end up like me, imprisoned here for the rest of your life."

I didn't dare tell her I had smoked for a few years before giving it up. Like many teenagers, I had thought it made me look cool and grown-up, but it just made me feel nauseous. I motioned to the oxygen tank beside her bed, but Granny waved her hand to indicate she'd tough it out.

Granny was a tough cookie. I know so little about my father's relationship with his mother, but Dad told me that she could be cross and hard on him. My cousin Twink said that Granny had been really mean to her mother, my Aunt Jackie. Nobody really knew why, just that Granny's mother had supposedly treated her the same way. Granny was stern even with me, so I was cautious around her. Still, I couldn't dismiss the fact that she had summoned me to Bermuda because she obviously wanted to help.

I settled into a chair beside her and spilled my story about falling ill and struggling with this debilitating fatigue. At the end of my tale, Granny chided me. "There are lots of people worse off than you. How do you think I feel imprisoned in this bed? Stop feeling sorry for yourself!" She then ordered me to bed.

I went happily — relieved that someone was taking me in hand and realizing how much I wanted someone to just tell me what to do. That began a comfortable routine for the two of us. I ate, slept, and read — Granny had a fulsome library of books from biography to fiction, and she advised me to make the best use of my recovery and read everything I could. (She was right. It returned to me a sense of accomplishment. I read one hundred books in that next year and a half, falling in love with authors like Charles Dickens,

Somerset Maugham, Oscar Wilde, Jean-Paul Sartre, Jules Verne, Ernest Hemingway, John Steinbeck, Mordecai Richler, and Margaret Laurence.)

Granny and I would convene twice a day at her bedside — after breakfast and after our naps at tea time. That was when she seemed to have the most energy and her breathing was less laboured. In short bursts followed by long breaths, Granny would tell me snippets about her life, including what I most wanted to hear about, her life with Billy.

"Your grandfather was a restless soul," she began one day. "One week he'd have ice blocks delivered to the door, and we would all have to take up ice sculpting. Another time it was soap carving."

I didn't say anything, but I was secretly pleased to learn this about my grandfather. I could relate, having always felt that I had a restless quality to my personality, like a wind that kept blowing. And I saw this in my father, too.

My grandmother stopped and looked at me over her bifocals as if to suggest that Billy could be quite a handful, but she did so with obvious affection. "He liked being spontaneous," she continued, telling me about a time when they were living in Montreal. Billy brought a group of homeless people right off the street and into the house for a nice hot dinner. I tried to imagine these unusual guests sitting at the grand dining room table with my grandmother's fine white linens and bone china, while she discussed how hard it was to find good help in those days.

"Imagine my surprise," Granny said — again with a mixture of pride and disdain. That was Granny's communication style — slightly scolding, superior. It was how, I reasoned, she maintained the upper hand.

My grandfather had grown up in the once-thriving port of Owen Sound, Ontario, located on the southwest shore of Georgian Bay. It is a city that hasn't grown very much since my grandfather's day, and it still boasts Billy Bishop as its most celebrated native son. In fact, Billy was the son of Margaret and Will Bishop, who was a lawyer educated at Osgoode Hall in Toronto and who became Owen Sound's registrar. Billy had two other siblings: an older brother, Worth, and Louie, his younger sister. It was Louie who wanted Billy to meet my Grandmother Margaret, hoping to impress her friend by having her handsome brother escort Margaret to the local dance on Saturday night.

While the Bishops were well off, they were no match for the high-and-mighty Eaton family, a fine point lost on my grandfather on hearing about a possible meeting between him and Margaret. "I don't need any more girls," is what he had first said.

Indeed. My saucy grandfather was already making the girls swoon with his confident swagger and slight lisp, a foible that made him sound sweet and sensitive.

When my grandfather was a boy, he lived in a wonderful old Victorian house that has since been turned into a museum in his honour. Some say the house is haunted as people have seen lights flicker, heard doors slam, and even heard voices at night — female voices it seems, so it's not likely Billy's ghost haunting the place (alas!). But as a kid, I loved visiting his childhood home and, especially, tracing my fingertips over the place where Billy coarsely scratched his initials — WAB — in the brick to the left of the front door on the veranda. (Billy's initials are now protected by a piece of see-through plastic to prevent erosion.)

That same veranda was, in fact, where my grandmother was invited to tea all those years ago, unaware that Billy was spying on her from the dining room window. He liked what he saw in the lively dark-haired, hazel-eyed young woman. As a result, the couple courted, and eventually Billy ended up proposing to Margaret before he went off to war in 1915, something my grandmother's father felt was a hasty move for two reasons. First, Margaret's father, who everyone called "Da Da" (and who my father said was a "real prick"), didn't think Billy would return from the war; and second, he didn't think Billy or his family was good enough for his daughter. That all changed, of course, when Billy came home a hero.

My grandparents' love story is hopelessly romantic — my grandfather wrote my grandmother literally hundreds of love letters over the next three years from both England and France — most of which my grandmother kept and apparently responded to, although, as far as we know, none of hers to Billy survived the war.

It cost merely a penny to send a letter overseas back then, and Billy's regular missives were hand-addressed to Miss Margaret Burden at 494 Avenue Road and often had the large "CENSOR" stamp on them indicating their contents had been read and approved for delivery.

Those letters belong to my cousin Twink now, locked up in a safety deposit box, but she has allowed me to read them and marvel, as my grandmother must have done, at my grandfather's unfettered adoration for his beloved Margaret.

Grandpa Billy, in uniform, with my grandmother, Margaret, 1917.

September 9th, 1915

My darling,

I think what it will mean when we are married, you will be mine, absolutely and solely my own. You are now, I know dear, but there is a subtle difference, somewhere, perhaps it is because you are mine in the eyes of the whole world when we are married. It is wonderful to think of those glorious days coming in our lives when night and day I can hold you in my arms and love, love, love you!

To every morning awaken to kiss you first thing and to feel you warm your lips on mine and hear you say, I love you. To even write this thrills me, my darling.

Margaret, with my heart and soul I love you, love you as a girl was never loved before, of one thing you may feel assured and that is, I shall never change.

Love to all, your fiancé Billy.

Billy married Margaret Eaton Burden on October 17, 1917, at Timothy Eaton Memorial Church in Toronto.

"I had the most beautiful wedding dress," my grandmother recounted as we looked at the photos from that day. We lingered longest over the one that had been published in newspapers around the world. In it the dashing Billy and his lovely Margaret walk arm in arm down the steps outside Timothy Eaton Memorial under a canopy of swords held up by forty officers of the Mississauga Horse regiment while throngs of onlookers line the street. My own heart leaped at this real-life fairy tale.

Billy's mother had given my grandmother one piece of advice about marrying her son. She said to Granny, "Don't try to push Billy. You've got to lead him."

I wonder if this was what she did. I think I would have sensed if my grandmother had been unhappy in her marriage. But she waxed authentically about their life together — the fun they had, the people they knew, and the parties they went to. She was clearly devoted to him. And while I could not bring myself to ask her, Granny also did not seem fazed by Billy's indiscretions.

Dad bragged that women fawned all over the war hero and that his father always had multiple lady friends, perhaps also a fling with a movie star or two, and I already knew how she'd handled that. Granny invited Billy's mistresses to lunch, and then supposedly watched him squirm.

Dad also told me that Billy did confess to my grandmother that he had taken a mistress in France during the war. It's interesting. In all the letters Billy wrote to Margaret, there's a gap in 1916 when there were no letters. We don't know if they were lost or if Granny conveniently dispensed with them. More likely the latter as it would have been around the time that Billy was in the doghouse over the affair.

To be fair, I wanted to believe that Granny had her own share of admirers and adventures, and she rewarded me one day with a story that suggested that she did.

As the granddaughter of Timothy Eaton, she had inherited and collected a lot of lovely things from jewellery to silver to antiques, but one item in particular had always fascinated me — a large silver pig that my grandmother displayed with great vanity as a centrepiece at the dining table. It was indeed a showpiece, crafted of pure silver, almost thirty centimetres high and half as wide. It came in two parts, and the head came off to expose a hollow middle. I couldn't imagine that there was another one like it anywhere in the world. I'd asked Granny where she got it.

"A gentleman gave it to me," she said.

"Granddad?"

"No, dear."

"Then who?" I asked, agog.

"Well," Granny continued, "Billy was off somewhere giving speeches, and I was dining with a gentleman friend of ours at the Ritz in London."

Granny let the innuendo hang there like diamonds dripping from a tiara. Her communication style was deliciously Jane Austen–like, in that what was implied was so much more important than what was being said.

I imagined Granny looking the essence of the twenties flapper in a pale pink beaded dress with one of those headbands to match. I could practically see her elegantly manoeuvring her black onyx cigarette holder, the one with the rows of small diamonds around it that I admired so much. I also visualized her dinner companion as a dark-haired man with eyes only for her, as inappropriate as that would have been with Granny being married and all.

"We were having a lovely evening catching up on friends and parties when the gentleman excused himself and left for what seemed like the longest time," my grandmother said, enjoying the fact that I was clearly spellbound. "I was beginning to think that he had abandoned me when, suddenly, he returned holding the silver pig."

"Where did he get it?"

"He had gone to buy it for me."

Then the obvious question.

"Why?

"I don't know, dear. I didn't ask him. But he then proceeded to order champagne."

My favourite part was coming.

"When the bottle arrived, my gentleman friend took the pig's head apart and poured the champagne into it. Then we took turns drinking from it — right out of the pig's head!"

It's the only tale that I remember my grandmother telling me that didn't include my grandfather. I loved it. I could also see that she enjoyed telling it.

The story always stopped there, though. Somehow, I knew not to ask what happened next. Maybe nothing. You didn't pry where Granny was concerned. Perhaps I also just wanted to believe there was more to the story. My grandparents' lives were my benchmark of what high society was like, and I wanted it to be complicated and full of intrigue. I understood that it was part of a bygone era, when people, and especially married couples, were expected to play certain roles. It was about as far removed from my own life and circumstances as anything could be, but I revelled in these glimpses of glamour, money, and prestige, and I always would.

Anyway, at that point, Granny picked up the book she was reading, indicating to me that we had now concluded today's conversation — and as if to say, "come to your own conclusions."

That winter in Bermuda with Granny was like being in a cocoon. I could have basked in her safe haven for a little longer, but I was getting stronger and I decided I was ready to go home.

I had arrived in Bermuda when both my body and mind had been in a state of limbo, shut down because I could not move forward emotionally. I had felt hemmed in, grappling with questions about what I should do with my life and the unconscious guilt of believing that I deserved a life of my own, even when my mother didn't have one. I have wondered ever since then whether that was the reason I had fallen ill.

As I got ready to leave, I felt I had a new resolve to find the answers I needed.

I cherished the time that I spent with Granny that season, which I might not have had otherwise, and I remember so well the day that I left her. As she sat upright in her bed, I kissed her goodbye and thanked her for giving me this precious gift. I had walked out of the room and was almost at the front door where Hugh was standing, ready to drive me to the airport, when I felt a sudden compulsion to see her one more time. I ran back. She had a look like *what's all this?* yet she didn't resist another long hug.

"I love you, Granny," I said.

"I love you too, darling," she replied, and then added what we used to say to each other when I was a child. Before I went to bed, she always said "Goodnight, Love," and I would respond the same again, "Goodnight, Love." (I couldn't help but think what a contrast it was to my father's nightly exits.)

That was the last time I saw my grandmother. She died almost two years later, my last living link to my grandparents' dazzling era.

CHAPTER 12

TELLING STORIES

Once I returned to Toronto, on my insistence, my doctor (Mr. Blank) referred me to some specialists, first an internist and then a doctor in tropical disease medicine, as it was suggested that with my travels with the airline, I might have contracted a parasite.

Fortunately, that was not the case, but I found someone who gave me some semblance of an explanation for my incapacitating state. There wasn't yet a name for it, but the doctor told me that a mysterious new condition had surfaced where patients were inflicted with persistent fatigue. He said they still didn't know much about the ailment, but it appeared to be hitting young people, and more women than men. Patients' immune systems were compromised initially by a flu-like illness, but the condition could also include other factors such as a prolonged state of undiagnosed stress.

The condition is now most commonly referred to as chronic fatigue syndrome, or CFS, and it was considered a controversial medical condition at the time (less so now).

There was no medication or suggested therapy to deal with CFS other than to give in to it and let the body heal itself. The doctor I visited believed CFS was more prevalent among high achievers, but I have never found any science to support this. Like my grandmother, the doctor was stern and gave me no pity. However, he seemed confident enough to assure me, "You will get better. I just don't know how long it will take."

There was great relief in having an actual diagnosis, to know that I was dealing with something real, and it let me give myself permission to recover in my own time instead of wondering if I ever would.

Even with this encouraging news, my father was still in denial that anything was or had been wrong with me. I think he really just didn't want to believe that his perfect "Pookie" could be less than perfect.

Unwittingly, however, it was Dad who offered me another lifeline to my recovery. In the process of restarting his writing career, Dad had an idea for a book that would eventually be published in 1998 called *Destruction at Dawn*. It was about a special mission called Operation Bodenplatte (German for "baseplate"), the last large-scale strategic offensive on Allied airfields by the Luftwaffe (German Air Force), which took place on New Year's Day 1945. Ironically, it was a story similar to my grandfather's solo raid on the German aerodrome (the one that won him the Victoria Cross) — only reversed.

Dad needed someone to begin research on Bodenplatte, and he offered to hire me to do it. It wasn't a subject that I would have taken an interest in normally — but I wasn't well enough to find full-time work, and I needed to do something, so I agreed.

So began my new routine. In the mornings, when I had the most energy, I went to the nearest library, only two blocks away, and delved into the history books. It wasn't long before I was enraptured, reading about how the Allies had been taken by surprise, still fast asleep in their beds, recovering from the festivities of New Year's Eve, as the German planes descended and attacked the airfield. Thankfully, there were few casualties on our side, and the Allies were able to replace their lost fleet within a week.

Through this task I rediscovered my thirst for knowledge. Once my work on Bodenplatte was complete, I kept going to the library every day, reading the newspapers and news magazines like *Time* and *Newsweek*. I was curious about the world and hungry to learn something new. I also discovered that I liked my own company and actually enjoyed being alone.

* * *

Like so many other times in my life, it wasn't long before my grandfather's ghostly presence resurfaced — a short time after I came back from Bermuda, the National Film Board of Canada approached my father about making a documentary about Billy Bishop, as a matter of public record. This had come about largely on the coattails of the success of a new stage production called *Billy Bishop Goes to War*, written by John MacLachlan Gray in collaboration with actor Eric Peterson, that had premiered to great national acclaim in 1978. The musical was such a success that it rekindled the Bishop legend and lustre, not just for me, but for the whole country.

The play portrayed my grandfather as a scrappy colonial who suddenly finds he is really good at something — fighting and shooting down the "Huns," as they referred to the Germans in World War One. I was mesmerized by Eric Peterson's tour de force performance where he plays not only Billy Bishop but over a dozen characters, both male and female, people who my grandfather had run across in his trajectory toward becoming a war hero.

My favourite was Lady St. Helier, the British socialite and friend of Winston Churchill's with connections and influence in the war office. She had been a pivotal figure in my grandfather's life, helping him make the transition from the trenches to the air, and Peterson was masterful in his chiding rendition of the elderly matron who took my grandfather under her wing.

> **Lady St Helier:** Bishop — you've been making rather a mess of it haven't you? You are a rude young man behaving like cannon fodder, perfectly acceptable characteristics in a Canadian. But you're different. You're a gifted Canadian, and that gift belongs to a much older and deeper tradition than Canada can ever hope to provide.*

It was thanks to the play that for the first time I got caught up in what it was like to be a pilot in the First World War. Peterson brought the battles to life. Holding a small model airplane, he animated the "dogfights" using his own sound effects, and you could almost imagine the exhilaration and sheer terror of what it must have been like to set one's sights on an enemy aircraft, getting in the first shot before being shot down.

I loved it. So did our whole family, although my mother and father assured me that Billy was very little like the cocky country-bumpkin

---

* From *Billy Bishop Goes to War*. Musical by Eric Peterson and John MacLachlan Gray.

character depicted in the play. Billy, they said, was rather soft-spoken and refined. He rarely used bad language. Even when he was angry, he apparently just puffed himself up and expelled an indignant "Well, well!"

Still, the show was highly entertaining and is still performed today as one of the country's most popular theatrical productions.

Having had such a wonderful experience with the theatre, we were really excited about the prospect of the documentary and being contacted by the National Film Board. My parents invited the director, Paul Cowan, along with his film crew, to breakfast one morning at our house. We never ate breakfast in our dining room except at Christmas, so it was pretty special to be doing so on this occasion.

I was still on the mend and was delighted to have some interesting company. I liked Paul immediately, and so did my parents. He talked about his passion for Billy Bishop, his childhood hero, and his enthusiasm for getting started on this dream project. He also told us stories about his other films and his fascinating life as a writer and director. He had recently been nominated for an Academy Award.

My father agreed to co-operate to the fullest and would go on to open up the family archives of documents and photographs as well as his own wealth of contacts and knowledge. Dad had spent a year researching his father's life and searching through records in both Canada and Europe while writing Billy's biography.

As for me, I was unabashedly entranced, as was my mother, by this intellectual and unassuming man with dreamy pale blue eyes. I was even more enamoured with his work and career, and this chance encounter caused an almost seismic shift in me, one that perhaps I was moving toward anyway. It gave me hope that I might have something to offer, something around which I could build my life.

I was discovering my love for telling stories. I had grown to understand that the process of making a film, or writing a book, even doing PR, was virtually the same: it involved deciding what story you wanted to tell, gathering the information and research, and then pulling it all together to weave a compelling tale. I was attracted to that process. It was a way I could express myself, put my stamp on things. It promised a life of constant learning — and possibly the adventure I craved. And it was right under my nose. My father had chosen a career in storytelling, whether through journalism, advertising, PR, or writing his books. Why hadn't I seen it before? Apparently, it took an impassioned speech from this attractive young man before I really took notice.

I wasn't sure what means or method I would find to be able to do this, and I didn't know what stories I wanted to tell, but I was curious and I could get interested in almost anything if I took the time to investigate and explore the subject — Bodenplatte had taught me that.

The NFB director never knew the effect that simple breakfast meeting had on me. Nor could either of us have envisaged the impact his film about Billy Bishop would end up having on both of us.

CHAPTER 13

COMING THROUGH FIRE

I had been struggling with chronic fatigue for two and a half years — an eternity for a twenty-something — but in the year following my diagnosis I finally started to recover my strength. The effects of those lonely and difficult years would stay with me, however, and I would always have to be careful not to overextend myself or overdo it. It took me longer to recover if I pushed myself beyond a certain point. This was very frustrating to explain to people who wondered why I needed to rest or why I said no to certain activities. Someone once asked me what I was saving myself for. I wasn't. I was just trying to keep up. Had I been a different sort of person, someone with a different family history maybe, I might have had the good sense to focus my life on something less taxing, but instead I picked a career that, with the effects of CFS, I should never have been able to do. I picked a trade that would take out of me all that I had to give it — the high-octane world of journalism.

I made the decision to go back to school and study journalism at Concordia University in Montreal. The idea of starting over in a new place, with a new focus, held real excitement for me.

In retrospect it seems obvious. Journalism was already in my blood. Dad had been a reporter, albeit briefly, and my brother Bill was studying at Ryerson's journalism school in Toronto. I, too, spent a year at Ryerson before deciding I should take advantage of my French and plant myself in a city where I could use the language. We were, in the end, a family of storytellers who would each find a unique way to use this particular faculty.

So there I was saying goodbye to Mom once again, but this time I knew I might not be back for a long time. As I loaded up a Rent A Wreck van with a bed and my few belongings, I felt as if I were abandoning her for real, even though my brother was still at home (though not for long). I wanted to say, "Mom, I am so sorry, but now I have to save myself or I will never get better." But she already knew that. Montreal wasn't that far away, anyway, I reasoned.

The other difficulty was that I was broke. All those years I'd been unable to work had eaten into my paltry savings. I had nothing left but my drive to succeed. The summer before I left for Montreal, I got a job as a clerk in a government office, a position that was not too demanding. I had also secured a student loan and a fellowship grant to be an English-language assistant to post-secondary French students in a Montreal CEGEP. The job paid me enough to cover my tuition. It also allowed me to eat, albeit sparingly. I rented a very tiny one-room apartment in an old dilapidated downtown house.

Nevertheless, I was euphoric. I was in Montreal, a city with a soul rich in architecture, music, and art, a place where people enjoyed food and wine as if every meal were their last. Local and provincial politics was standard lunch and dinner conversation, and there were always so many things to talk about and debate. These were heady times in *la belle province*. Quebec had survived twenty years of both exhilarating and exhausting political transition. The separatist Parti Québécois (PQ) and its charismatic leader René Lévesque had come to power but had been thwarted in their mandate for separation in a first referendum, and, as a result, the party was losing some steam. Montreal in the early eighties was showing signs of economic stress. Several of the country's big businesses had moved their head offices out of province, and there had been an exodus of many in the anglophone community. People were touchy and cranky — a dream environment in which to study and work in journalism.

I was soaking all this in, but moving slowly. I was still pretty weak, managing only three or four courses, and I would often spend my afternoons taking a long nap. Still, it was progress.

I loved journalism school, and especially broadcast journalism. Gloria Bishop (no relation), who eventually ran CBC Radio, was one of my first professors there, and she made it come alive for me. On the very first day in her class, she plopped us down, one at a time, in front of a microphone in a radio studio and told us, "You have one minute. Tell me why you want to be a journalist."

When my turn came, it just all spilled out. "My name is Diana Bishop. I am from Toronto. My story is simple. I have been unwell, and now I am picking myself up and starting over. The only way that I can think of to do that is to do something new. I am tired of my own story. I want to hear other people's stories, and I want to help people tell their stories."

It sounds super corny to recall those comments now, but Gloria smiled and said, "Welcome to my class, Diana."

After less than a month in Montreal, I was settling into my new life. However, around midnight one night after I had gone to bed, I thought I was dreaming when I heard someone scream, "FIRE!"

I woke out of a dead sleep to see thick black greasy smoke curling its way underneath the front door of my apartment.

"FIRE!" another female tenant called again from downstairs. "GET OUT! The house is on fire!"

Barely awake, I sprang into flight mode. The smoke was seeping in under the door with such alarming intensity that I had to think fast. I had the wherewithal to grab my contact lens case, a pair of old running shoes, and my wallet before running for the fire escape. Thank God there was one. I looked back at the thick black smoke enveloping my tiny room.

About ten minutes later when the fire engines arrived, the old house, pretty much a student slum, was beyond saving, gone along with everything I owned, which admittedly wasn't much. I had one prized possession that in my haste I'd left behind — a mahogany makeup and jewellery box that I had inherited from Granny Bishop. One of the treasures from her youth, it was quite large and beautiful, lined with navy blue velvet, and it held myriad compartments with silver-topped bottles for lotions and creams.

There is nothing like a fire to make you realize that all you really have in life is yourself — a lesson I thought I had already learned from being so ill. Naturally, I was in shock as I stood outside watching the curious crowd gather and wondering what in heck I was going to do.

I was fortunate to have a cousin living nearby who put me up, and the next day I walked downtown to Eaton's with my one credit card. I bought a top, a skirt, some underthings, and a pair of shoes, all in dark colours so they wouldn't show the wear because I knew they would be all I would have for a while.

I waited a day before calling my parents, once again feeling guilty about worrying them. I had put them through so much already, and now, finally, after setting out on my own, I was adding more drama to their lives.

Admittedly, I was relieved when they decided to come to Montreal for moral support. Mom went back to the scene with me to pick through the charred remains and we made an astonishing discovery — Granny Bishop's jewellery box had survived the fire. It was singed and needed a major cleaning, but it was basically intact.

"Your grandmother is watching over you," my mother murmured. Yes, now I had both Granny and Billy watching over me.

My father took us out for dinner at the Ritz-Carlton on Sherbrooke Street, where my parents were staying, not too far from my now demolished abode. I was heartened by my parent's visit because I knew they couldn't really afford it. What a deliciously insane contrast it was to be dining on escargots and crème brûlée when I had only one outfit to my name. Instead of a care package, my parents thought they should comfort me with dinner out at the best restaurant in the city — that was just how they did things. And there was something else. I got the sense that the occasion allowed some little part of them to relive their glory days in Montreal in the fifties— when Billy and Margaret were still alive and resided nearby, and they all probably met for drinks quite often at the Ritz.

So I savoured every mouthful, and I didn't dare ask my parents for money. It didn't seem right to impose on them any further. Besides, I knew I would find a way to make it all work.

And I did, thanks to friends and my extended family — my cousin John Aylen, who provided me with a place to stay until I got back on my feet; and his parents, Aunt Andree and Uncle John, my mother's brother, who lived in Ottawa and sent me more than a few care packages. I will always be indebted to them for that.

Eventually, I was able to get a new apartment, and while I finished up my degree over the next couple of years, I landed a plum job with CBC Television in Montreal. For someone just starting out, and very green, it was beyond my wildest expectations to find myself in the heart of a big-city newsroom that had a reputation for pumping out some of the finest broadcast journalists in the country. It was an environment with a daily diet of fires, murders, demonstrations, hunger strikes, and out-of-the-ordinary political stories — such as a PQ minister who was caught shoplifting a fur coat from the downtown Eaton's department store, or the francophone family who complained that their mother, who had been treated in an English-speaking hospital, had not been allowed to die in French.

Local TV news is fly-by-the-seat-of-your-pants stuff, where you are expected to do research, set up interviews, go out and get the story, then write and edit it — all in the space of about eight hours. And woe betide you if you miss your slot on the six o'clock newscast. I don't think I took a full deep breath at all those first few years. Being the new kid, of course, I was expected to pay my dues, working ridiculous hours (every weekend shift for almost two years), and sometimes having to file two different reports a day for both the 6:00 p.m. and 11:00 p.m. broadcasts.

I don't think anyone suspected the physical toll it was taking on me. I didn't let on; in fact, I ignored it as much as possible. With CFS still hovering over me, as it has for much of my life, I pushed myself as far as I knew I could, and spent any time off sleeping and resting to prepare for another week. I curtailed my social life, my circle of friends, my romantic attachments — anything to allow me to continue this wonderfully exciting, stimulating job.

I was exhausted most of the time. It cost me a lot. I was a sprinter in a world that demanded a marathon runner. It was another secret I was keeping, and I had decided it was worth it. Even my parents didn't know; this was Billy Bishop syndrome at its most potent.

I was also delighted to do any story I could get, of course, but I admit, at first, I found myself shying away from the big stories. I was terrified of failing, and I worried that I might not be good enough for this new career. One of my first stories was covering a fire. There was an arsonist on the loose in Montreal wreaking havoc with backyard sheds, with the fires often spreading to people's houses. Fires are easy stories to report on. All you have to do is show up and ask questions. In this particular case I talked to the fire chief, some of the neighbours, and then to a man whose family had lost their home and their belongings. With my direct experience, having recently lived through a fire, I think my face registered compassion that the interviewee was not expecting. He took one look at me and broke down and cried — on camera. As my edited report played through the CBC newsroom at 6:00 p.m., one of the seasoned reporters remarked. "Well, Bishop, you made him cry. You will go far in this business."

But that was my only foray into hard news for a while. That first summer and fall, I was assigned mostly human-interest stories — those reports considered soft news and not journalism at all, but rather more like entertainment. Every local newscast needs them to fill in the gaps on the slow news days. In these situations I thrived and showed off my gift for storytelling and being able (like my father) to make any story sing — such as when a big moose got loose in downtown Montreal. Poor moose, he had somehow made his way into the city and, under the duress of the hot pursuit of the provincial authorities and a pack of overzealous reporters, finally jumped into the St. Lawrence River. It took a Herculean effort by animal rescue, but the moose was eventually shot with a tranquillizer gun, hoisted onto a flatbed, and transported back into the woods.

I edited my report to the music of *The Charge of the Light Brigade*. It was written up and praised in a French media magazine as "creative reporting," and from that day forward I was, for better or worse, the most worthy candidate for the animal beat.

I followed the story of two peregrine falcons (then an endangered species) that returned every year to nest and hatch their chicks on the ledge of a skyscraper, fifty storeys up. I even did a story about three mallard ducks whose fluffy little fannies got stuck to the ice of a nearby river during a spring thaw. I was able to milk the story for three whole days. In fact, my reports generated a national following over that period and ended up being the lead story on the first broadcast of CBC's new noon show called *Midday*.

Of course, I couldn't hide from the big story forever.

On March 24, 1985, there was a mass murder at the Hells Angels' Lennoxville clubhouse in the Eastern Townships. Two months later the bodies of the five Hells Angels members shot to death at the clubhouse were discovered at the bottom of the St. Lawrence, wrapped in sleeping bags and tied down with weights. It was dubbed the Lennoxville Massacre.

One of the more seasoned reporters had claimed that story, which began with a preliminary hearing in the Montreal courthouse. But then she got sick, and they decided to send me instead. I was terrified. This was the Hells Angels, for Pete's sake. It wasn't a story about squirrels.

With that trial by fire, I became the lead on a story that lasted several years, with all sorts of dramatic twists and turns, the most exciting of which was when the judge announced that one of the jurors had to be relieved of his duties. Why? Because he had been "bought" — Juror Number 12 revealed that he had been offered $25,000 by the Hells Angels to swing the jury toward an acquittal.

Going to court for months on end was daily theatre. I faced the stares from bikers with names like Zig Zag, Snake, and Tiny (who was anything but), who sported telltale tattoos like the "Filthy Few," ink that was, according to reports, worn by members who have killed for the club. It was gripping, and I finally pinched myself. I was doing what journalists called "hard" news; in other words, *real news*.

In those early days when I did reports that became national news, and the Hells Angels certainly fell into that category, my parents watched, my mother so thrilled for me and my new career, and my father and me bonding over the fact that we both loved the news business.

Dad never talked much about his time as a reporter with me. We didn't share or swap stories because frankly, at this time in my life, we didn't see or talk to each other much. I came home for the big holidays like Thanksgiving, Christmas, and Easter when I could actually get away, and in the summertime I would always try to book a holiday somewhere with my mother. I cherished our time together, and it seemed the least I could do to rescue her from my father once in a while. Dad didn't complain. I think he also knew that Mom might need a break from him.

When Dad and I did speak about journalism, we talked about the times when Dad tried to "stir up a little shit."

For example, while at the *Windsor Star*, Dad felt that the paper needed to beef up the letters to the editor, which were, at that time, relegated to the back pages of the newspaper. As a bit of a lark, Dad composed a letter that took direct aim at veterans coming back from the war (which, keep in mind, he was one himself), taking all the good jobs, and still "strutting around in their uniforms." Dad's editor got wind of it, read the letter, and decided to print it. It caused quite the stir, inspiring thirty-one furious replies — a record for the paper — and turning Dad into a bit of a hero as readership soared. You certainly couldn't get away with anything like that in my day, but it did make me chuckle.

I continued to dive into my work and a dizzying blur of events that grew more compelling and spectacular as I rose in the journalist ranks.

I spent five years working as a general reporter for CBC's local newscast *Newswatch*, where, for a while, I was the crime and court reporter. Tensions were also running high over the language issue in Quebec, and there seemed to be daily developments in the restrictions of the rights of Quebec's anglophone community, which kept our newsroom humming. I became Quebec City's bureau chief, covering politics in the Quebec National Assembly, a highly coveted posting and rite of passage for any serious Canadian journalist. The highlight of that year was an election; I went out on my first campaign trail and got to co-anchor the live election-night coverage.

In that same year, 1989, I heard that CTV was looking for a reporter to fill an empty position as a national parliamentary correspondent in Ottawa. I applied for it and got it — making the huge leap from local reporting to the national political arena. At first, of course, I was completely overwhelmed and in way over my head. I was shoulder to shoulder with Canada's elite of TV news correspondents at that time — Craig Oliver, David Halton, Jason Moscovitch, and Wendy Mesley — and felt unworthy.

The events of late 1989 and the first half 1990 also turned out to be two of the most action-packed years I ever had in the news business.

There was the tragedy of the Montreal Massacre, when on a very cold day in early December an enraged lone gunman shot and killed fourteen women at Montreal's École Polytechnique. Later came the fall of the Berlin Wall, the execution of Romanian president Nicolae Ceaușescu, the Meech Lake constitutional crisis, Nelson Mandela's release from prison, and the beginning of the Gulf War, all of which took place within a period of about eight months. I worked so hard, travelled so much during those few months. Life was, quite frankly, off the charts.

There were a couple of insane days when I completed a report for CTV's eleven o'clock news with Lloyd Robertson, jumped on a plane at daybreak the next morning to Newfoundland to witness then–premier Clyde Wells cancel a scheduled vote on Brian Mulroney's ill-fated Meech Lake Accord in his provincial legislature. Covering this turning point and filing reports both for the *National News* at 11:00 p.m. and for *Canada AM* the following morning, I got to bed around 2:00 a.m., grabbed three hours of sleep, then headed back out to the airport to catch the first flight back to Ottawa. Racing into the capital, I put in another full day of filing reports marking the ultimate death of the Accord, then collapsed into bed well after midnight.

Without so much as a day off, I sprang back into action, covering Nelson Mandela's historic visit to North America, Canada being the first stop on his list, and then I covered the Queen's visit. Right after that a Quebec provincial policeman was shot to death over a land dispute with the Mohawk nation in Oka, Quebec, near Montreal. That began a standoff that would last months. Arriving at the scene in the afternoon after the shooting, I filed several taped and live reports. I was looking forward to a hot bath and a few hours sleep in a soft bed in my hotel, but it was not to be. Provincial police had set up roadblocks and wouldn't let anyone back into the area once we left. For the next couple of nights, my crew and I slept in our cars as the temperature dipped to 10 degrees Celsius. Wearing the same clothes for a few days and having to pay surrounding home-owners to use their bathrooms was not fun, but I survived that crisis, too.

I was run ragged, but there was no question I was in my element, happily playing out my restless nature with one new adventure after another.

The few short conversations I had with Dad during those years were typically about the funny or unusual things that happened while I covered a story.

I had Dad in stitches over the time that I was in Kennebunkport, Maine, covering a brief summer meeting between Prime Minister Mulroney and U.S. President George Bush Sr. I had filed a report for the eleven o'clock news and stayed up to prepare one for the next morning's *Canada AM*, finally going to bed about 3:00 a.m. Then around 6:30 a.m. the phone rang in my room. There was no air conditioning, as it was a very old hotel, so there I was lying on my bed ... well, naked.

I picked up the receiver and it was the Toronto office. "Can you do a quick phone interview with Pamela [Wallin] about what's going on there, Diana?" a producer asked. It was a rhetorical question. Before I could reply, I heard the countdown: "five, four, three, two, one ..." Pam's voice chimed in: "I have Diana Bishop on the line from Kennebunkport, Maine, where we understand that the prime minister and the president are out early fishing — Diana, can you tell us what they are up to this morning?"

I am a professional, of course, but I was naked, and feeling just a bit odd that I was about to go live on national television while lying on my bed. I also had no idea if the two leaders were actually out fishing, or just frying up a plate of kippers back at the Bush compound, so I glossed over their current whereabouts and talked for a minute or two about what we expected during the day ahead.

My father got a big kick out of that story because it sounded like something that might have happened to him. And I was pleased that he was enjoying my adventures — meeting and interviewing the newsmakers of the day, doing what I loved, and living this extraordinary (definitely not ordinary) life.

CHAPTER 14

No Way to Treat a War Hero

The very first report I did for Remembrance Day caused a bit of a stir.

Remembrance Day is one of those occasions that journalists cover every year, like the Canada Day celebrations. Like most reporters, I got the opportunity many times, but I also think some of my editors thought it might be interesting to have Billy Bishop's granddaughter fronting the report — whether or not viewers would make that connection.

Remembrance Day is a solemn ceremony held at cenotaphs in Commonwealth countries at the eleventh hour, on the eleventh day, in the eleventh month — the exact time that hostilities ended in the First World War in 1918. It pays tribute to those who have fallen and those who have served and continue to serve their countries with comforting rituals — including two minutes of silence, a bugler playing the "Last Post," and the laying of wreaths.

It is a straightforward assignment, but the first time I covered the ceremony, when I was just starting out in Montreal, I felt I had the weight of my family background on my shoulders.

I thought perhaps something more was expected of me than just describing the details of the Remembrance Day event, so I ignored many of the familiar formalities and tried to personalize the story. I approached the attending veterans, many of whom, like my father, had served in the Second World War. I asked them to tell me about someone they lost to the war and what they remembered about them on this day.

Most answered in a detached way with the same narrative that my father had always given me — they'd all suffered and lost compatriots. I was gentle but direct on this day, and one or two opened up, broke down, and wept in front of me. One told me that he had watched a fellow pilot get shot down and crash over enemy lines, another about a bunkmate killed by a sniper's bullet right next to him in the trenches. My report focused on the individual stories of these men, a detour from the usual script.

I was naive, I know. I didn't realize I had broken their stoic code.

I was trying to get at a layer of emotion that I had not been able to crack with my father or his buddies, so it came as a surprise to me when the telephone lines lit up after my story ran on the local six o'clock news — veterans calling in, incensed that I had dishonoured them by not sticking to the usual script.

I was stricken that the callers felt that I had betrayed them, but I was even more distressed that I couldn't articulate what I had really been trying to do. I wanted to give them an opportunity to tell the real story. I believed it took guts for these few veterans to open up to me the way they had, and I wanted to showcase that courage. It had backfired, and I guess I felt betrayed, too, that the callers thought I had done veterans a disservice.

To further complicate things, a couple other events happened around this time. Montreal appointed a new chief of police, and I was tasked with interviewing him. It was a standard interview asking him about his new role and so on, but when we finished and the camera crew was packing up, the chief looked at me and asked if by any chance I was related to Billy Bishop, the flyer. I was so proud to tell him yes right off the bat, and then a sudden bad feeling overtook me — he was a cop after all! I asked, "Why?"

His answer was not what I expected. I thought he might say that he knew my granddad and tell me what a great guy he was. Well, yes and no. As a young cop on the beat, he had known my grandfather in the fifties, and he was a fan. In fact, Billy had lived just up the street from the police station at which he had worked. Then, rather affectionately — I will give him that — he said to me, "Your grandfather used to get very drunk. We would find him staggering around, so we brought him in and put him in a cell until he sobered up. Then we let him out and he made his way home." From the way he put it, it sounded as though this happened more than once.

I don't think I really processed this information right away. But it hit me like a body blow. Up to that point, anything that I had been told about my grandfather just elevated him in my estimation. I accepted that he could be a bit of rascal at times because I could imagine him being so, what with the twinkle in his eye that was so apparent in his photographs.

But this story was sad and emotionally charged. I couldn't get my head around my grandfather being anything but perfect. Up to this point I had never allowed him to be human. To think of him in decline and not living up to his former life of heroic glory was heartbreaking. Had my fabled hero just fallen off the pedestal I had put him on? I wasn't sure. Harder still to stomach was that Billy's drunken behaviour reminded me of Dad. Alcohol was not just Dad's demon; it was a family demon. Even more upsetting, I suddenly became aware that, so far in my life, I had carefully separated my grandfather and my father. One was my hero and the other my anti-hero. I'm not sure why I had needed to do this. Perhaps I was trying to bring some order to the family role models I had grown up with, and I needed to see things as black or white. Anyway, whatever had just happened, it felt like a turning point.

It was not long after this encounter that my grandfather became national news once again with the release of the National Film Board documentary. The press it generated didn't turn out to be what my family or I had expected.

There was one hint, a red flag that Dad mentioned briefly to me: he told me he was a little concerned after being interviewed for the film by Paul Cowan.

"The NFB might be trying to take a different approach about my father," he said to me one day. When I pressed him for details, he said, "They are out to smear him, I think."

He didn't elaborate. I didn't push. It is just the way we were as a family. Of course, there was no reason for me to be interviewed for the documentary, but I had spoken with Paul a few times over the course of filming. In fact, he had very kindly kept in touch with me while I was ill. However, he didn't mention anything to me that might indicate a change in his attitude toward my grandfather. Or at least I don't think he did. Frankly, I was still so star-struck by the director and the influence he had had on my decision to start a career as a journalist that I might not have been listening carefully enough.

The NFB film was called *The Kid Who Couldn't Miss*. I assumed that the title referred to my grandfather's uncanny shooting ability. I couldn't have been more wrong.

Paul invited me to be the first of the family to see the documentary. Was it a calculated decision to test it out on me? Likely. I was closer to the director than the other members of my family. But I also was the only one in my family who lived in Montreal, where the NFB had its head office and where Paul had summoned me to view the screening along with his colleagues. Initially, I was thrilled to be asked, but as I took my seat in the small screening room, I remembered what my father had said and suddenly felt very nervous.

As soon as the lights dimmed and the nearly eighty-minute film began, I got a sinking feeling. From the start the production had the subdued tone so characteristic of NFB films — but in this case the narrator's cadence took on the beat of a slow drum marching a man to his execution.

Banking on the popularity of the theatre production, *Billy Bishop Goes to War*, the documentary had videotaped segments of the play and included them — but only the more serious and melodramatic scenes where my grandfather, portrayed once again by actor Eric Peterson, reflected on his internal fears about war and the devastation it was causing.

In between these segments, it continued to paint a dreary and humourless picture of my grandfather as the poorest of prospects to become a member of Britain's Royal Flying Corps (RFC), let alone a war hero.

The film built slowly for a while before it finally dropped the bomb that would ignite a bitter controversy.

Forty-eight minutes into *The Kid Who Couldn't Miss*, the director did an interview with a former First World War pilot by the name of Cecil Knight. Paul asked Knight if he had ever heard anything about Billy Bishop being a fraud: "Cheating on his kills" is how Paul put it, quoting a source. He explained that the source was another former British First World War pilot who had been interviewed about his war experiences but had since died. Paul had discovered the audiotape in the Imperial War Museum archives in London, and in it the pilot apparently made a few derogatory remarks about my grandfather.*

---

* H. Clifford Chadderton, *Hanging a Legend: The NFB's Shameful Attempt to Discredit Billy Bishop, VC* (Ottawa: War Amputations of Canada, 1986), 198. In a transcript from the senate subcommittee on Veterans Affairs, Paul Cowan testified that the interview he listened to at the Imperial War Museum had been a former Royal Flying Corps pilot, Archibald Henry James, KBE, MC.

Cowan quotes what Mr. James said in the recorded interview: "But of course, the best known and most advertised [pilot] was Bishop, the Canadian. Unfortunately, Bishop was fraudulent. He began very well and was genuine, but he was so ambitious to have the highest total that he began claiming successes that were completely mythical."

Paul Cowan to Cecil Knight: He [the pilot on the tape] thought that Bishop was a very ambitious man and was cheating on his kills and that it was generally known in the RFC that Bishop was cheating. Had you ever heard that?

Cecil Knight: Never. [He says this quite emphatically, and then pausing, continues] I doubt it. It was not in the character of Bishop as I knew him to do a thing like that.

Despite his forceful response, the exchange was the beginning of the documentary's gradual unravelling of my grandfather's reputation. The film alleged that Billy Bishop might not be the hero that everyone thought he was — that he may not have shot down seventy-two planes, that instead, he had exaggerated his score and made some of them up.

The potential loophole that lent plausibility to the film's theory was my grandfather's habit of going out alone in the early morning before dawn to look for the enemy, a signature tactic that earned him the nickname "The Lone Hawk."

The NFB's film made it sound as though Billy chose those solo missions so no one would be around to witness his victories. In particular, the NFB took direct aim at my grandfather's most famous raid, the one for which he was awarded the Victoria Cross — that day on June 2, 1917, when Billy single-handedly attacked a German-held aerodrome — the first time such a manoeuvre had ever been attempted.

This is what my grandfather wrote in his autobiography, *Winged Warfare.*[*]

> I planned this expedition after much thought, and set it for the second of June, as that was to be my day off. Dawn was the hour I considered advisable, as there would be very few machines in the air and I would have a great chance of evading trouble on the way to the aerodrome.

My grandfather recounts that he had trouble finding the specific airfield he was looking for and thought of packing it in. Instead, he just kept flying

[*] William Avery Bishop, *Winged Warfare* (Toronto: McClelland, Goodchild & Stewart, 1918), chapter 15.

low in the hope of finding some other action. That's when he discovered the sheds of another aerodrome.

"Another half minute and I was over the aerodrome about three hundred feet up. On the ground were seven German machines, and in my first glance, I saw that some of them had their engines running."

And so, as he tells it, began his extraordinary battle. My grandfather pointed the nose of his plane down and flew over the aerodrome, scattering bullets across his path. As he dodged machine gun fire coming from the ground, Billy then opened fire and downed one plane and then another as they attempted to come up to meet him. By that time two more machines had taken off but in different directions. Billy engaged the one heading straight for him and, after a couple of circuits around each other, he fired one short burst, sending the enemy aircraft crashing to the ground. Billy emptied his final drum of ammunition on the fourth machine but failed to hit it before he hightailed it out of there.

Making it back to base with his machine shot up badly, Billy wrote later, "I landed, and my sergeant immediately rushed out and asked how many I had bagged. When I told him three, he was greatly pleased and yelled it back to the mechanics who were waiting in the shed."

The next day, in one of his letters to Granny, Billy recounted the exciting highlights of the attack while seemingly underplaying its consequences:

> I didn't write to you yesterday. I had a busy day. I rose at 3 a.m. and flew over a hun aerodrome where I did a very cunning battle in the way of shooting.... I now learn I have been recommended for the VC which I won't get I'm sure ... three letters from you today, 3 wonderful love letters, all my love, your fiancé, Billy.

That was what I knew and had read about the raid before the NFB film, which was making the case that it never happened.

The NFB director did not include in his film any actual evidence or sources to prove his theory; however, he also didn't find any evidence to prove that the raid happened as Billy described it. That was the problem. There were no official records of the attack — on either side. Billy had no witnesses, and any records the Germans might have had were destroyed in the Allied bombings during the Second World War.

The glamorous Margaret Bishop, my grandmother, poses for a portrait in the 1920s.

For Paul Cowan this opened the door to doubts that it had ever happened and the possibility that Billy had made the whole thing up. In order to spin his theories, Paul had staged a dramatization, a fictitious scene in the film where an actor (coincidentally, once again Eric Peterson) pretended to be Billy's airplane mechanic. Adopting a strong Cockney accent and forming a small circle with his hands, the actor says, "In the tail [of Bishop's aircraft] there's about seventeen bullet holes, all in a group.* I have seen a lot of planes shot up, but nobody can shoot up a plane like that, you know. Quite a mystery!"

In other words, the film was positing an alternative theory of events that suggested that Billy had landed somewhere and shot up his own plane to make it look like he had been in battle before returning to base.

For some reason, Paul had not played the tape recording of the pilot that he had found in the Imperial War Museum, nor did he include on-camera interviews of the two other sources he found in England who raised doubts

---

* There are varying reports about the extent of the damage to Billy's plane when it returned to base that day.

about Bishop's record.* It was also not clear if Paul had tested his theories on Canadian military historians or people who had known Billy as there were no interviews to that effect in the film whatsoever. I suspect that my father may have been asked about the allegations during his interview, but Dad did not tell me about that, nor did Paul.

As a result, when *The Kid Who Couldn't Miss* ended, it left me hanging. I didn't know what to think. I wasn't expecting these unsettling allegations, and I didn't know what I was more upset about — the fact the film had raised them without proof, that it had used misleading and confusing methods to raise speculation (as it was sometimes hard to distinguish fact from fiction in the film), or that the documentary presented such a lacklustre rendition of my grandfather's life — while not perfect, he was anything but dull.

As the lights came up, Paul's colleagues warmly applauded and lined up to shake his hand in congratulations. As an outsider, all I wanted to do was leave as fast as I could, but as I moved toward the exit, Paul approached me to ask what I thought. He looked tentative. I was tongue-tied. I'd had no time to digest what I had seen. How could I process the implications of something that had blindsided me in little more than an hour? That the NFB had vilified my grandfather, a Canadian icon, was crushing. As well, I was crushed in another way: I had idolized the NFB director, but in an instant he had fallen head first off my pedestal. I was running out of heroes.

All I remember was muttering, "I think my father is going to be upset," before making my escape.**

---

* Chadderton, *Hanging a Legend*, 199. Paul Cowan says he personally interviewed two other people in England — former pilot Willie Fry, MC, who had flown with Bishop and was there the day Billy returned from the June 2 raid; and Joe Warne, a former No. 60 Squadron Leader (Billy's former squadron). According to Cowan, both men raised doubts about my grandfather's record but neither appeared in the film.

** I was so glad my Grandmother Bishop never saw the NFB film, nor was she around to hear of the controversy. She died on March 27, 1981, while the documentary was still in production.

CHAPTER 15

HERO OR FRAUD?

I still cannot quite grasp what transpired as a result of a few lines in a film that, quite frankly, few Canadians would ever see. But they didn't have to. Once the media got wind of the film's contentious approach, headlines started to appear in the national newspapers, making the NFB's handling of the attack of my grandfather's famous raid a focal point.

"Billy Bishop, Hero or Fraud?"

"Air Ace Held As Liar"

I wince to think that if I had been the journalist covering this story, I probably would have sensationalized it, too, but I was also the granddaughter, and it was a reminder of how much my family story was a part of me. Our most cherished member was under attack, being maligned. This turn of events united our dysfunctional family in a nanosecond. We burnt up the phone lines trying to make sense of what was happening.

My father was livid, of course, and I believe deeply hurt. Any mention of the NFB during this period sent him into a rage, and we were not allowed to bring up the film director's name in his presence. Publicly, Dad didn't discuss the allegations, nor did he feel the need to defend them. He thought that would just add fuel to the fire. But privately, he cursed and swore. He ranted. And for once I was sympathetic. It did seem so unfair. Billy was not here to defend himself and the NFB was attacking the man my father looked up to more than anyone in the world, the man in whose footsteps he had followed so completely.

"Dad, you wrote a book about your father. You did your own research. You know what really happened. Why won't you speak out?" I pleaded.

"Nobody will ever believe the family," he replied. "No matter what we know or think, people will say we are biased. We are better off to stay out of it."

Behind the scenes, however, Dad had many admirers and supporters, and consequently he didn't have to be the one to defend his father's name. A groundswell of Canadians voiced their outrage that a government-funded institution could betray a national war hero. It came primarily from veterans like Cliff Chadderton of The War Amps, who compiled a book called *Hanging a Legend* condemning the film, as well as from related organizations such as the Canadian Fighter Pilots Association, the Air Force Association of Canada, the RCAF Prisoners of War Association, and the Royal Military Colleges Club of Canada, just to name a few. Some journalists and many individual Canadians took up the charge with columns, petitions, and letters to the editor calling the NFB film a national embarrassment.

The furor grew so strong that, by 1985, some key players like Senators Jack Marshall and Hartland Molson (of the Canadian beer family and a personal friend of Billy's), both war veterans themselves, took up the fight with a vengeance, prompting a senate subcommittee to undertake a study into the activities of the National Film Board in relation to the production and distribution of *The Kid Who Couldn't Miss*.

It was a rigorous and often acrimonious debate. I truly believe that when director Paul Cowan raised doubts about my grandfather's war record, he had no idea of the strength of the backlash that would follow. Nor do I believe he set out to make a negative film about Billy Bishop. As he claimed in the hearings, he tripped on some information (albeit mere rumours) that he believed he could not ignore. But I felt — and I *am* putting my journalist's hat on here — that his portrayal of my grandfather's life, including the handling of the contentious raid, was misleading and unbalanced. I thought the fabricated scene with the mechanic was a really cheap shot. I think Paul had been naive — not fully appreciating that taking on a legend with so very little to go on would be seen as an attack on all war veterans.

During the Senate hearings, I was still in Montreal working for the local CBC newsroom — thankfully far enough away from Ottawa, where the "Billy Bishop" story was raging, to stay out of the spotlight. Surprisingly, my journalist colleagues didn't question me about it much, and I adopted my father's attitude that talking about it wouldn't do any good, anyway. Never during this period did I have a conversation with anyone in my family about the possibility that the allegations might have some truth to them. I didn't dare. My family was ferociously loyal, and their image of Billy was untouchable.

Then there was the bigger picture. At the time I was mystified as to why this was happening some sixty-five years after my grandfather had served in the war. That is, until I really thought about it. My grandparents' and parents' view of the world wars was one of supporting the noblest of causes. Households were filled with families whose sons had literally run to join up for God and country. There was an almost hysterical patriotism that they were going off to beat the Germans and save the world.

Growing up, as I did, with television had brought the reality of conflicts like Vietnam right into our living rooms and, with them, a sense of disillusionment. We were also a generation the majority of whom had never seen active combat, never had to defend our country, and never thought much about the fact that, were it not for what our fathers and grandfathers did, we might not even be here.

I viewed this explosive debate as a thinly veiled clash between transitioning generations — those that formed the deep bond of having experienced and survived the two world wars, wars they believed in, and where the word *honour* really meant something; and the next generation that questioned more and dared not take war, or even heroes, at face value. In fact, wasn't that what my innocent first attempt at a Remembrance Day report had been all about? To blow the veneer off what had already been hidden, hashed, and rehashed the same way for so long. But I also questioned after this debacle whether my generation could revisit those previous generations' histories and rewrite or rework them with our altered perspective. How could we possibly know or understand what they had really been through unless we had experienced it in their time?

This was the essence of the debate that ensued between the NFB and members of the senate subcommittee, and where I found myself sometimes appreciating both sides of the story.

The following is an excerpt of an exchange between Paul Cowan and the subcommittee chairman (Tuesday, December 10, 1985: Subcommittee on Senate Affairs, October 17 to December 10, 1985):

The Chairman: Mr. Cowan, the last time you appeared before our committee you made a statement, and I am paraphrasing, "The country needs its heroes, but I think a country should be skeptical about them. They make war more simple and glorious than it is."

Why should we be skeptical? Am I misquoting you?

Mr. Cowan: I think that that is right. I think the flyers in World War One are a very good example of that. When we think of flyers in World War One, we think of these young, daring, romantic boys flying around with silk scarves trailing out of the back of their airplanes. We never think of them dying or killing people … one of the images from the First World War is clearly that of an unsullied ace who somehow goes out and never gets blood on his hands and is never hurt himself and conducts a rather sanitized war. It is just not the case.

The Chairman: You cannot be skeptical about the servicemen who went overseas. You cannot make something simple that actually existed.

Mr. Cowan: I am not trying to make it simple. I feel that heroes have been made to be rather simple … it is more complicated than that … when one becomes a hero, there are all sorts of pressures that come to bear, which, for the average fighting sod fighting in the trenches, for instance, never existed.

I was also drawn to another exchange, this one between the then-commissioner of the NFB, François Macerola, and a senator during these same hearings of the senate subcommittee:

Senator Lang: When this film was released, was it, in your opinion, in the national interest?

Mr. Macerola: Absolutely, yes.

Senator Lang: And what was that national interest?

Mr. Macerola: As I said previously, to ask pertinent questions with respect to being a hero in this country.

Senator Lang: In other words, you are asking the question, "Do we really need heroes?"

Mr. Macerola: Yes.

In the end, the Senate could not censor the film or ask to have it destroyed without trampling on obvious democratic freedoms, but it did recommend it be labelled as a "docudrama" due to its use of fictional characters and scenes.

As a result, the NFB agreed to add this scroll at the beginning of the film: "This film is a docudrama and combines elements of both reality and fiction. It does not pretend to be a biography of Billy Bishop. Certain characters have been used to express certain doubts and reservations about Bishop's exploits. There is no evidence that these were shared by the actual characters."

This, of course, leaves you wondering *what the heck does that mean?* Like saying this film is about something that might not have happened, but it might also be about something that did. *Huh?* It seemed such a preposterous conclusion to an exchange that had cost a great deal of taxpayer money, aired so much venom, and seemed to sully and embitter all of the players. The NFB was clearly shaken. The senate subcommittee was criticized for publicly demonizing the director, coming very close to stomping on the right to free speech. And, of course, at the core of the whole mess was my grandfather's reputation, which had been tainted, perhaps irrevocably.

But what did I really expect? That the film board and Paul Cowan were going to call to apologize? That would have been great, actually, but it was a fantasy. And so I was left with a grey area, an unfortunate hole in my grandfather's record. Nothing could repair that except undeniable proof, and it did not seem to exist.

It had all felt like a tempest in a teapot, even as the uproar died down, but questions about my grandfather's war record still hung in the air like a bad smell. I remember standing in a group of people at a party, and someone introduced me to a CBC producer of some standing, who said, "I understand you are Billy Bishop's granddaughter!"

After all that had happened, I was on alert when I heard this, but before I could reply he added snidely, "Well, I guess he is still a hero to you, eh?"

The room went quiet.

"Well, yes, in fact he is, you SOB!"

That's what I should have said.

But I didn't. I had been caught off guard, yet again. I just smiled and excused myself. Inside, though, I was furious with that SOB, but also with myself. Why hadn't I said something? Why couldn't I stand up for myself and speak up? That's when I realized that, despite my attempts to look at the whole issue objectively, as I had been trained to do as a reporter, I had taken the attacks on my grandfather personally. And why wouldn't I? Anyone would expect me to defend my grandfather. My grandfather had made such an important contribution to the war and to his country, and people had called him a liar. They had questioned his integrity, and that, I reasoned, must mean that they were questioning mine. We were cut from the same cloth, weren't we? I had been brought up with a certain image of Billy that I never questioned, and I had built my self-worth around trying to be like him. But I didn't really know my grandfather, did I? Everything I knew about him came to me second-hand. He wasn't real. Billy was a ghost, and he was certainly haunting me now.

CHAPTER 16

THE FAMILY SECRET

In 1992, after three years covering national politics and international affairs as a parliamentary reporter in Ottawa, I scored a plum posting as CTV's first full-time female foreign correspondent and Beijing bureau chief (where I eventually also worked for the American network NBC News).

It was a period of my life when I lived on pure adrenalin and was more determined than ever to prove myself. I was stronger physically then, but still driving myself hard, making up for it by getting as much rest as I could on my time off.

Whether it was because of the grandfather I had or the interesting people who had come through our home when I was young, I relished being around great people. There are few other professions where an ordinary person can be consistently in the presence of extraordinary people.

Being a journalist allowed me to meet, interview, have lunch or dinner with, or be among a small group in the same room with Canadian prime ministers from Pierre Trudeau to Jean Chrétien, world leaders like Nelson Mandela, U.S. presidents George Bush Sr. and Bill Clinton, Russian president Boris Yeltsin, Chinese president Jiang Zemin, celebrities like Mary Tyler Moore, Michael Douglas, Céline Dion, and *Titanic* director James Cameron. It was about more than appreciating their accomplishments; I was captivated by what motivated and drove them, and by their vulnerabilities. Prime Minister Brian Mulroney needed to be liked; Clinton needed to feel a connection; Céline Dion couldn't believe how far she'd come; and James Cameron thrived on the hunt — he was an explorer.

As China bureau chief for CTV and then NBC News, Beijing, 1992–96.

Interviewing Canadian prime minister Brain Mulroney in Paris, 1992.

Probably my favourite encounter, though, was meeting the Queen at a Commonwealth Summit in Zimbabwe, during which I was whisked away by her handlers when I attempted to grab her hand and gush. She reminded me so much of Granny Bishop that I just couldn't help myself. I was naturally drawn to famous people. It was in my blood. My life was intense, exciting, interesting, and intellectually stimulating, and I happily lost myself in other people's stories. It was also far away from worries about my parents' lives, where so little changed. Well, a few things had.

My parents had moved again during this time. They now had a lovely old upper duplex in an even more stylish part of Toronto (but still a rental, naturally). It was affordable for them because the building was owned by their friends Chink and Gill Fleming. Mom dressed up the new residence with the usual turquoise paint, but this time cushy matching broadloom gave the whole place a tropical feel. The Flemings lived downstairs, which was nice for everyone, especially at cocktail hour. During the summer months when I was home for a visit, I could usually find them all having drinks in the backyard on what became known as the "Raccoon Terrace."

"Damn raccoons, they follow us everywhere," Dad chortled.

Over the years, Dad had wound down his PR business — most of his clients were retiring anyway — and he now had time to work on his real passion: writing. It had been years since Dad had written his father's biography, but his interest in Canadian military history had expanded. My father read everything he could find on the two world wars, and his knack for packaging stories came in handy as he chronicled real tales of Canadians who had distinguished themselves while serving their country. Dad was a populist at heart and wanted our military history to come alive to the average person. He was a thorough researcher and very prolific, and I believe Dad had at last found a place to channel his emotions about the war. It was a successful career for him in that way, although not a particularly lucrative one. His books were popular, but his market was small, so writing never made him enough money to live on.

That became evident when Dad suddenly stopped paying the rent but didn't say a word about it to my mother.

"How did you find out?" I asked.

"Gill told me," Mom said, looking humiliated.

"And what did you do?"

"What do you think I did? I paid it!" my mother huffed. And she never said anything about it to my father. She didn't talk to him about it. He didn't talk to her about it. They just carried on as if nothing had happened. My mother simply continued to pay the rent.

A number of years earlier something similar had happened. Dad had defaulted on a loan at the bank, and the bank had taken out what he owed from my mother's account. It wasn't a large amount, but really — they could do that in those days! Outraged, my mother walked into the bank the very next day and withdrew her money, depositing it with the competitor across the street.

Since that time Mom had received a small inheritance from her parents, which she guarded with her life as it gave her the only sense of independence that she had ever known. She wasn't making any money. She was living only on what my father gave her to run the household, so it must have killed her to have to use her inheritance in this way. Still, she said nothing. Instead, she went out and got a job.

It was at times like these that I was flabbergasted by my mother's strength of character. At age sixty-five, the daughter of a Harvard-educated lawyer, the wife of the son of Billy Bishop, was taking shifts at a second-hand clothing store and earning minimum wage. My heart broke for her, but there was something about this new experience that rejuvenated her — a sense of freedom perhaps? Mom was really enjoying being in the company of other people and it seemed to revive her.

After she'd had a number of different retail experiences, my brother was kind enough to offer my mother a desk job at Bishop Information Group, a marketing business he and a partner had started that specialized in working with highly motivated entrepreneurs. That, along with some financial help here and there from me to make sure that my parents had what they needed, took some of the pressure off.

I am not sure if my father was ever as direct with my brother, but one night when I was in town, my parents took me out to a restaurant. My father suddenly laid his knife and fork down, looked me right in the eye, and said, "Do you know how proud we are of you?" I was stunned. Both my brother and I were doing well, and I guess it must have been gratifying for them to see us using the communication and marketing skills that we learned from and practised with them.

My brother had married, had a son, divorced, and then found a new partner, to whom he was later married. I, on the other hand, was still single. This has always been difficult for me to talk about, and my parents, thankfully, were among a small minority not to prod or question me about such things. My mother never harped, as some mothers do, about the suitability of my boyfriends, or the big wedding she would organize, or all the grandchildren she hoped she'd have. We never discussed marriage or children at all, actually. Instead, she wanted to know about the stories I was covering, the places I was getting to see, and the interesting people I was meeting. I felt my mother wanted me to have the life I was leading. Perhaps she was living a little through me — as a woman single-mindedly following her dreams and passions unencumbered and uncompromised by a husband or children.

In truth, though, I suppressed any of those thoughts by becoming a workaholic. After being ill for those few years I felt I needed to make up for lost time, and my career was my safe place, my comfort zone. It was the lens through which I developed a sense of self-worth. The harder I worked, the better I got at my job, and that gave me a measure of control. It was never enough, though. There is a saying among journalists: "You are only as good as your last story." Editors like to keep you on edge with that provocation.

But that's also how I was living my life — a proverbial carrot always dangling in front of me, urging me to do better. No matter how successful I got, I never felt successful.

I had fallen in love with a few Prince Charmings, and some had developed into longer-term relationships. I admit I really had a wonderful time with them. They were all highly intelligent, determined men — some were journalists, one was a diplomat. And that was the problem. They were just as ambitious as I was. Though I thought I should want marriage and a family, what I valued most was my independence, and I think they sensed that — perhaps even better than I. So with all of them, sometimes after a few months, others after several years, I came to a fork in the road. I reasoned that they didn't want to keep me from my career nor I from theirs. But I also figured they understood that I wasn't "marriage material" and just didn't want to admit it.

I did, in fact, both crave and fear love. I had been traumatized by my parents' relationship, and I was terrified of finding myself in a situation where I felt trapped, the way my mother seemed to be with my father. I had watched my mother wither, losing herself little by little. It horrified me. And it seemed to happen to me once I got into a relationship. I would start to feel that I was losing a part of myself, making someone else's world more important than my own. It was not a risk I was willing to take. As a result, it was far easier to keep an emotional distance from affairs of the heart, remain emotionally unavailable (while secretly harbouring feelings of being unloved and unlovable), and choose men who were very good at doing the same.

I didn't realize any of this until my late thirties, after a relationship I had with a married man (and yes, that one was guaranteed *not* to work out), when I admitted that I needed help. I asked my family doctor for a referral, and she sent me to a psychiatrist who specialized in helping children of alcoholics (COAs).

My doctor must have seen that connection, but I had still not put two and two together. In these sessions with the psychiatrist, I learned that I had many of the classic signs of COAs — the approval seeking, an overdeveloped sense of responsibility, chronic anxiety, and an addiction to excitement.

That last one took me by surprise. The chaos of growing up in a home where there is constant turbulence can cause you to expect it even when it is no longer present. I learned that, in its own way, my background could induce a form of post-traumatic stress disorder. Interesting, then, that I would have picked journalism as a career; news, and especially TV news, with its often-tragic events, ultra-fast pace, and heart-racing deadlines, is by definition a daily drama that can become like an addiction.

This was a lot to take in — and I couldn't for a while. Remember that my generation had grown up with a muddled definition of an alcoholic. That was until one particularly intense session when the psychiatrist, a very gentle, soft-spoken man, asked me, "Diana, tell me this — if your father had to choose between you or a bottle of Scotch, what do you think he would choose?"

Such a simple question. And my answer was automatic. "The bottle of Scotch, of course."

Had I really said that? Did I really believe that?

Pieces of a puzzle that had long been floating around in my head suddenly started to snap together into a clearer picture. It was the first time I admitted to myself that my father was not someone who just "drinks a lot," as I had been taught. Yes, my father had some control. He set a timetable around when he would start drinking, but the truth was he still drank every day and he drank until he got completely blotto. That made him what is called a "functional alcoholic" or "high-functioning alcoholic," but an alcoholic all the same, and that meant he was sick. He had a disease. It also meant that I would never come first in his life. I cried and cried.

I continued therapy and I said nothing about it to my parents. Self-preservation, really. I did not even want to think about what my father would say. I knew he wouldn't get it. My mother knew, but I could see it made her uncomfortable, worried perhaps that in the course of therapy I would find reasons to blame her for my problems.

It was enough for me just to keep going to work. I had so much to process, observing myself through this new filter. Then, just as I needed a change, something happened — as things so often do — to put me on a new path.

CHAPTER 17

A Hero to Me

I had been working for almost fifteen years in TV news, a most reward-ing career and one where I met a lot of fascinating people and travelled to different parts of the world. Then, in 1997, I was once again back on Parliament Hill working for CTV, which had graciously hired me back after my return from abroad. Two and a half years into that job, CTV did some downsizing. As last in, I was first to go. It was the right move for both parties. I no longer belonged there, and they knew I wasn't happy. Fortunately, just before that happened I was being courted by Global Television to be their new Senior Parliamentary Correspondent, so after I was fired, I simply walked from one building to another, gaining a promo-tion and a new deal.

Global had agreed to let me do more in-depth feature stories, work that I believed suited me better creatively, and they took my interest in doing something for their documentary unit seriously. It didn't take me long to come up with an idea that Global embraced immediately: I proposed a documentary on my grandfather. I would call it *A Hero to Me*.

Making my own documentary, a personal documentary about my grandfather, was a reflex. The controversy over the NFB film and that pro-ducer's comments stayed with me and, eventually, became a catalyst to chal-lenge me. "Take that, you small-minded, arrogant CBC producer!"

Yes, maybe the thought of redemption played a part in my deci-sion, but looking back, I think I was still trying to figure out for myself

Me, in a promo shot for my documentary, *A Hero to Me*. I dedicated the film to the greatest unsung hero in my life: my mother.

whether my grandfather was indeed a hero to me. And also why in heaven's name this was still so important for me to figure out.

In deciding to explore my grandfather's life for myself, I thought I could just see where I ended up. That was it. I had no formal agenda. I now understand, however, that my subconscious was at work and that I couldn't hide forever from my suppressed feelings and thoughts.

It made sense to start with what I was ready to learn. What would it have been like to be among the first to do combat in the air?

The stars aligned to help me with this project in so many ways. I had a wonderful director, Craig Thompson, whose first task was to find a way to recreate some First World War flying scenes. That's how I ended up in a farmer's field one hot, sunny summer's day — looking skyward — watching two First World War flying machines engaging in mock aerial combat.

The first was a biplane like the one my grandfather flew — a full-scale replica of an S.E.5a with the two red, white, and blue roundels on either side. A closer look would reveal my grandfather's name embossed on the left side: "Flt Lt. William Avery Bishop, Victoria Cross."

The second plane was gleaming red with the telltale black-and-white rimmed crosses on the side and the tail — also a full-scale replica, but of a Fokker Dr.1 triplane. The Germans, including the eminent Red Baron, flew this aircraft in the First World War.

It was thanks to my grandfather's many devotees that the Great War Flying Museum, part of the Brampton Flying Club in Caledon, Ontario, had graciously loaned the aircraft to us for the day along with seasoned pilots Earl Smith and Jerry Fotheringham.

The grass field served as a landing strip where a group of First World War re-enactors from the 20th Battalion Re-enactment Group had also volunteered their time to set up a camp just like it might have been during the war. They brought flags, tents, rifles, and uniforms, all authentic right down to the last detail.

As I watched the S.E.5a (Billy's plane) take off to tackle the Red Baron, I felt that I was being transported back in time. I gazed up and gawked at the two vintage machines dipping and diving in and out of manoeuvres while Geof Richards, the cameraman who had worked with me in China and whom we'd hired to shoot the film, leaned precariously out of a Piper flown by another big Billy Bishop fan, pilot Barry Lewin. As Barry circled the action, Geof recorded the footage, and cheers erupted from the ground as Billy's plane roared past, bearing down on the enemy, missing him by a few feet, and then climbing back up to a better vantage point.

"That was close!" I found myself saying out loud, lost in the realism of the moment. The planes danced around each other, almost like a ballet at first, and then Billy's plane veered up again, bearing down on his opponent with a round of (fake, thankfully) ammunition. This move was called a "suicide dive," and Billy was famous for it.

It was such a rush. I closed my eyes and listened to the whirling purr of the biplane engines. I could imagine the sensation of being airborne in 1917, manoeuvring a 130-horsepower machine, travelling faster than anything ever had before — me at the controls peering through a tiny windshield, scouting every inch around and above me until I spied the enemy. I felt fear mingling with the exhilaration of anticipating a dogfight — where I would surely be the *vainqueur* and not the victim. It was intoxicating like a sport or a video game — and yet for my grandfather, there would have been real bullets coming at him, and he, too, was aiming his guns right at the enemy's head.

"What would it have been like for Billy flying in one of these aircraft?" I asked Earl Smith afterwards. I wanted to know more about the rigours of flying in the First World War, especially in these fragile machines made of little more than wood, canvas, and wire.

"Well, for starters, Billy was flying less than fifteen years after the Wright brothers made the first flight."

A flight that lasted a mere twelve seconds.

"Aviation was in its infancy. The engines of these biplanes were unreliable and could quit at any time," Earl continued. "They were oiled with castor oil, and the fumes flew back into their faces, often making the pilots ill and giving them diarrhea."

Earl also explained to me that the flying scenes he and Jerry had done were about a thousand feet above the ground, while my grandfather engaged in combat ten times higher than that and sometimes in temperatures well below freezing. "They carried spare ammunition drums and often had to change them in mid-flight," Earl said. "Can you imagine trying to change those drums with the stick between your knees, with hundred-mile-an-hour winds hitting you in the face — all the while you are getting shot at?"

No, I couldn't. But there was so much more. I learned that the average lifespan of a fighter pilot in the First World War was about ten days, even shorter in April 1917, the bloodiest month for aerial combat and the month my grandfather started flying missions. In fact, most of the pilots who flew in the Great War did not survive. (Even the greatest ace of all, Germany's Red Baron, was eventually shot down and killed.)

The average mission took about an hour, as their aircraft had to get back before they ran out of fuel, and most did less than one sortie per day. I learned that my grandfather often went out two or more times a day, sometimes alone at first light, then again with his squadron, and sometimes he even went out on his day off. This blew me away. If Billy's plan was to increase his score by putting himself in harm's way more often, this was certainly the way to do it, but at what cost? First World War pilots were being shot down faster than they could be replaced, so it struck me as a terribly risky and reckless strategy considering his odds for survival. If that didn't tell me something about Billy's psyche, I don't know what would.

And what about the whole idea of keeping score, anyway? I learned that all of the pilots wanted to increase their scores; they all wanted to kill as many "Huns" as they possibly could. It was war, after all, and they got more medals that way. It was what got them up in the morning and kept them from dwelling on their probable demise. They were the first knights of the air. They were young. They made it a game and were competitive with one another. I can certainly see why my grandfather might want to be the best of the best. That's what I would have wanted to do.

Our tight filming schedule ended up coinciding with several unexpected events and made me think that someone "upstairs" was guiding me along in this project. Could it be Billy himself? I hoped so.

The first coincidence was that the city of Owen Sound, Ontario, where my grandfather grew up, decided to celebrate the eighty-fifth anniversary of my grandfather's June 2 raid on the German aerodrome. (Really and truly, I did not plan my documentary around this event. We learned of it as we were mapping our filming schedule.) It couldn't have worked out any better. On another glorious summer day, an Air Force band played, and dozens of young air cadets paraded in front of the Billy Bishop Heritage Museum, my grandfather's former home. There was a day-long fair with an air show at the local Billy Bishop Airport, where I got to meet and talk to dozens of people of all ages. Visitors to the event shook my hand, told me how proud they were to meet a relative of the famous man, and peppered me with questions about what it was like to be his granddaughter. It was hard not to take all the attention to heart. I felt like a celebrity. But I was really touched to see these people, all these Canadians right in front of me for whom Billy Bishop was a hero, and whose minds could not be changed by anything negative that they had heard or read about him.

His fans had not been deterred even when, in a second coincidence, someone launched a fresh assault on my grandfather's reputation at the same time that I was making my film.

Billy Bishop was once again in the news. This time a former historian from the Department of National Defence, Brereton Greenhous, had compiled a new tome about my grandfather called *The Making of Billy Bishop*. Greenhous's work slammed my grandfather's record in great detail, dissecting each of Billy's victories, surmising that they largely came from unsupported claims. While the findings were once again circumstantial, with a heavily biased approach, the author concluded that Billy Bishop was a brave flyer, but also a "bold liar."

It was the last straw for my father, who publicly blew his stack and opened up to the media. I was racing to work in a cab one morning when I glanced at the front page of one of the national newspapers and saw a defiant-looking picture of my father (at that time in his seventies) above the fold. Underneath it was the headline: "BULLSHIT! Says Billy Bishop's Son."

The picture reminded me of the way my little brother used to intimidate his friends with a description of our father: "My Dad is mean, *real* mean."

I laughed out loud. I remember thinking, *Good, go for it, Dad!*

For Dad, when it came to his father, there was no grey area. Billy was his champion — then, now, and always.

While I wondered what I was going to do about this new assault, a third unanticipated filming opportunity suddenly presented itself. I was invited to record a public debate about Billy Bishop between Greenhous and another respected historian and author, Lieutenant-Colonel David L. Bashow, who took on the role of defending my grandfather. The liveliest part of the debate centred on the aerodrome raid, and while it shed no new evidence on the whole affair, it was both an educational and a spirited discussion, and it provided me with something that I could not have foreseen, even in my film — an opportunity to confront the enemy.

After the debate I approached Mr. Greenhous, a rumpled looking man in his early seventies. I planned to nail him with what I was really feeling about everything that had happened: "Hey, buddy, how does it feel to bring down a national hero? One who can't defend himself and who also means so much to me and my family?"

But, once again, I choked a little bit. I shook my head and gently sputtered out "You know, we are so hard on our heroes, and part of that is great because we need to be skeptical sometimes, but ..." and then I hesitated before starting again. "But in the end [pause], do you feel you have done a disservice? I mean, we need our heroes."

Before I could finish, Greenhous shut me down. "No, I think he [your grandfather] was a terrible liar and a cheat. But he was also a brave man. You can be both, you know!"

I thought about that comment, and no, I did not believe one could be that brave and also be a liar. It didn't make sense to me. But before I responded, my cousin Twink (also Billy's granddaughter), who had accompanied me to the debate, jumped in. Her blue eyes firing darts at the armchair warrior, she spat out, "I wouldn't discredit your grandfather!"

Everyone laughed, even Greenhous.

It cleared the air for a minute, but I was stuck with the same old nagging question: What do you do when a person you love and have held up to a higher standard, above everyone else, has been accused of something when there is no magic bullet to silence the allegations once and for all?

It was time for me to find my own truth.

I put myself into reporter mode and looked at the other side of the story. That is, rather than going on the defensive to try disprove the allegations, I played with the idea that Billy had embellished some of his claims and faked the June 2 raid. As purported by his detractors, Billy would have had to land, dismantle the gun on the fuselage, shoot up his plane to make it look like he had been in a dogfight, and then get back into the aircraft to fly home (assuming that my grandfather still had some ammunition left, as he says he emptied his final drum back at the German aerodrome).

Was I crazy, or did that seem hard to fathom? Consider that if Billy had done so, he would have been a sitting duck, an easy target for enemy aircraft out looking for prey.

I had also learned in my research that it was not a good idea to turn off a First World War flying machine if you needed to get back into it quickly. The rotary engines in use at the time idled at such high power that they could not be stopped unless the engine was shut down. That meant that if you kept the engine running, the plane kept moving. And if you turned the engine off without a mechanic nearby, it was unlikely that you could get the machine started again on your own.

I tried to visualize that — that while Billy kept his plane idling, he lifted his automatic machine gun (what was called a Lewis gun) off the fuselage (no easy feat either, I was told), jumped out, and ran after the plane to shoot it up. He would then have had to climb back into the moving aircraft, all the while hoping no one was around to take a shot at him. It boggles the mind. It would be like watching a cartoon. Looking at things from this perspective, it was laughable, and decidedly more logical to me that it all must have happened the way Billy said it did.

But even that wasn't the deciding factor for me. After all the research I had done for my documentary, it was something that my Aunt Jackie, Billy's daughter, said during her interview with me when something big finally clicked.

"I just don't think my father was capable of such a magnificent lie," my aunt finally blurted out.

A magnificent lie — that he had faked the raid that earned him the Victoria Cross.

My goodness, yes. Something so utterly unassuming could hold a simple truth. I had never considered that it would have been a magnificent lie for my grandfather to keep all those years — his whole life, in fact, and all to himself. Imagine him never telling anyone. Not even my grandmother, who would surely have scolded him relentlessly. And besides, Billy had not even been very good at keeping his womanizing a secret, had he?

Does it still bother me that I can't disprove the allegations once and for all? I would love to be the one to have done that. The rest of my family seemed to dismiss it all and move on more easily than I. I could have forgiven my grandfather for chasing women and drinking too much, but I couldn't have forgiven him for lying. He would be a fallen hero to me if he had lied, and that would have hurt, seriously hurt. It does not jive with the kind of man who would write 365 letters to my grandmother during the war, be a rock for my mother in her hour of need, and stand naked and exposed outside his front door as a lark. My grandfather was no saint, but he never pretended to be. He was pretty transparent. And I think this would have been far too big a lie to keep to himself for forty years.

Making the film underlined something else for me — that my grandfather would be no less a hero to me if he had shot down fifty instead of seventy-two planes. Because what I had come to respect and value about my

Billy Bishop was not just his score, but how good a fighter pilot he really was. He was one of only a handful of aces of his ilk who had stayed alive. He survived despite the fact that he stayed in the war longer and went out on more missions than almost anyone else. However, even more significant to me was how he dedicated himself after the war. Here was a man who had reached the climax of his life at age twenty-three and would have to spend the rest of his life living up to his own legend. My grandfather brought the same determination in his battles in the air to his life after the war — from the fun he created at every opportunity and the kindnesses he extended to people around him, to his dedication to building the Royal Canadian Air Force, tirelessly recruiting pilots for the Second World War and developing a fighter training program for the entire Commonwealth. He was not only a brave flyer but also a man of great devotion and commitment, unrelenting in his sense of duty and service to his country.

A Hero to Me ran on national television for a number of years in both English and French. It had two successful premieres in 2003. The first screening was organized by the Billy Bishop Heritage Museum in Owen Sound and played to a packed hometown audience in the main theatre. The viewing began with the fanfare of a marching band streaming down the aisle before the lights dimmed.

The other premiere took place in Ottawa at the beautiful theatre in the National Archives. My family, friends, supporters, journalist colleagues, students, members of Parliament, and representatives from National Defence, the Canadian Armed Forces, and the Canada Aviation and Space Museum all attended.

As I got up to thank everyone who had helped me make the film, and all those who had also come to see it, I was overwhelmed with emotion. I knew my film wouldn't change anything. It wouldn't appease my grandfather's detractors or erase their doubts. But it had changed and inspired me. Most importantly, it reinforced that my grandfather will always have many more fans than foes.

CHAPTER 18

DEDICATED TO THE ONE I LOVE

I dedicated the film to the greatest unsung hero in my life: my mother. After the final credits at the end of *A Hero to Me*, I had added a picture of my beautiful mother and the dates 1925 to 2001 because, sadly, she died before I started making the film and did not get to see it.

Nobody ever expected that my father, with the way he drank, would outlive my mother. But then some say the caregiver usually dies first, and my mother had certainly been that, selflessly tending to but silently resenting an abusive and alcoholic husband.

In early 2001 I noticed my mother was becoming fragile. She had always been determined to keep up a good front — she would rather have died than admit what she was going through with my father — but she was weakening, emotionally as well as physically. Her face could not hide her fatigue. She was tired of life, her life.

Mom could still get enthused about things outside her world, and she had always been my champion, so very excited about the idea of my making a film about Billy.

I was working on Parliament Hill when my mother called me. It was a humid Friday night with a slight chill in the air, the promise of the imminent end of the summer. "I am not well, Diana," she said with an air of resignation. "I think you better come home."

I wept on and off for four hours in the car as I drove along the highway to my parents' home in Toronto. I had made the trip so many times before, but this time was different. I knew my mother would never ask for help unless something was terribly wrong. I felt a nagging guilt that I should have connected with her more often, more than the two hours I spent with her on the phone on most Saturday mornings, and more than the regular trips home for special occasions. With my punishing schedule, that was all I seemed to have time for, but perhaps that wasn't the whole truth. I think I had started emotionally weaning myself from my mother in her final year, feeling intuitively that I was about to lose her, and needing to prepare myself to face life without her. That's how I protected myself from pain. I withdrew.

When I arrived home and saw my mother lying in bed, her belly extended as if about to give birth, I knew it was bad. She was diagnosed with ovarian cancer the following week.

It made we wonder about the theory that prolonged unhappiness could take root and grow in people as a cancer. I didn't want to believe this, but it rang true in Mom's case. Her sadness had been a slow burn.

"I will be dead in four weeks," she said in her matter-of-fact way. She seemed almost relieved. I was shocked, and told her so.

"No, no, I am relieved," she said emphatically. Money had become so tight in my parent's household that my mother had developed a morbid fear of finding herself old, sick, penniless, and out on the street. "Well, now I don't have to worry," she exclaimed. "I won't end up with a walker or in a wheelchair or having to wear diapers," she said.

As such a strikingly attractive woman, my mother, I knew, had dreaded old age. She feared the inevitable deterioration and the loss of power her natural attributes had afforded her during her life.

A few days before she died, I visited my mother in the hospital. She was still lucid but fading in and out of a drugged slumber. I was in dutiful mode, numbed by the sheer terror of losing the person who meant the most to me in the world.

"How's your father?" Mom asked, resting with her eyes closed.

"He seems fine," I replied although I really didn't know. I had dropped everything to take care of my mother. I had even told my boss at Global Television that I might have to quit if it turned out to be a long haul.

When my mother was still at home with us, my father stuck as close as possible to his usual routine — writing, going to the club, playing tennis, drinking in the evening. When Mom went into the hospital, Dad did his shift with her. We all took turns. When I arrived, I would usually find him silently sitting in a chair next to her, head down, doing a crossword puzzle. I don't know if they talked about what was coming.

During those final days, I sat on the bed with my mother, sometimes crawling in to lie beside her. I held her hand and I told her how much I loved her. I told her how grateful I was for all that she had done for my brother and me.

"Remember the time you brought home Melvin, the little kitten, in your purse? Bill and I were beside ourselves, we were so excited," I said to her. My mother had made this sacrifice even though she suffered severely from asthma, and we finally had to find another home for the cat after about a year. "Or the time we all went to Canada's Wonderland and you went on the roller coaster with us?" It had been our mother's first roller coaster ride ever and she was in her sixties. I remember her shoulder-length grey-streaked hair flying around from the force of the ride. Mom had looked so frightened, though she assured us she loved it and wanted to do it again.

I was never sure how much of what I said she heard, but I kept talking, anyway. I reminded her of all the fun trips we had taken together, those few weeks each summer when we had driven, just the two of us, down to the east coast to St. Andrews by-the-Sea and stayed at the summer home of Lord (Shag) and Lady Shaughnessy. In the presence of a couple who clearly adored my mother, she came back to life.

"I cannot remember a single time in our lives when we were ever mad or cross with each other — can you?" I asked, not expecting an answer.

But then Mom did answer me, her eyes still shut. "You know we made the best of it, Diana," she said, bringing my gratitude monologue to a sober halt. "I can't say that I love your father anymore, but I still like him. We had fun and he made me laugh." She paused then before adding, "Your father loves you very, very much, Diana, but I am sorry to say that he may become your problem now."

I started to take that comment to heart a few nights before she died. We had been keeping a vigil by her bedside in the palliative care section of Toronto's downtown St. Michael's Hospital, talking over her body as if she were listening to us and as if the most terrible thing we had ever confronted was not about to happen. By this time my mother had slipped into a coma and had started the regular pattern of haunting breathing that they call the "death rattle." Still, it was reassuring to hear her breathe, even in this distorted way. My beautiful mother lay unconscious, starting to go cold as life drained from her extremities, but for the moment she was, at least, drawing breath, earthly bound, and therefore still with me.

Even as he faced the loss of the woman he had been married to for more than fifty years, or perhaps for that reason, Dad was trying hard to be a source of comic relief. He wandered the hallways and made himself quite at home, as if he were staying in a five-star hotel and was in need of room service. I was set up on a cot beside my mother, and Dad had found an empty bed in a room down the hall. It was getting late when he suddenly appeared in the doorway. Dad had a cross look on his face, one with which I was all too familiar, as though he were about to give my mother hell because he couldn't find what he was looking for.

"Goddamn it. I can't find my pajama bottoms."

He was standing in the hall wearing only his underwear.

I could hear my mother's voice coming out of my mouth. "Oh, gaaawd, Dad! You can't wander around the hospital like that!"

"Well, shit, I can't find my pajama bottoms, and I know I brought them."

"It would almost be better to go naked than wear those awful things," I barked back at him. God, he could make me mad — not to mention that he was always in need of new underwear!

"Ah, come on, nobody here cares what my underwear looks like because they're all half dead."

I was used to his shock tactics and they weren't always funny, but I knew that Mom would have laughed at this attempt at black humour. Dad's irreverence was one of the things that my mother secretly admired about him. I started giggling. So did Dad. Somewhere inside her listless body, in that world between here and the hereafter, I hoped Mom was also chuckling to herself. I felt she was.

I was alone with my mother when she died the following evening — exactly four weeks after her diagnosis, as she'd predicted. Her chest heaved slightly as she took her last deep breath; and was it my imagination or did I feel her body expel its life force? Did I see some unknown entity — could it have been her soul? — float upward? Moments after, all that was left was a sunken shell.

Death is surreal, frightening to think about, but to see it, watch it, is oddly beautiful and reassuring. I felt I witnessed the essence of my mother going somewhere else, moving into another dimension. The thought uplifted me and gave me hope. And I couldn't help but also think, *she will be up there with Billy and Margaret now.* She would like that.

But then there is the void that follows. Who loves you like the person who gave birth to you? Who or what fills that emptiness?

My father burst into shuddering sobs over Mom's deathbed. But strangely, not in life nor at this moment, in death, did he touch her or kiss her forehead, not that I saw anyway. Not as I did once everyone had said their final goodbyes.

I remember leaving the hospital with my brother and father, heading back in the car to my parents' home, and looking around at other people on the street. It was very late. It had been raining and the streets were slick and shiny as people in cars whizzed past. My mother, the only one I would ever have, was dead. Her world had stopped, and mine, too, for a moment, but theirs just kept on going. It seemed wrong.

I can also say, though, that in addition to the great sorrow of losing my mother, I felt relief. My brother Bill has said he experienced the same sentiment. Our mother was free. And so were we. A burden had been lifted. We didn't have to carry around her unhappiness anymore. This was a new awareness for me, and one for which I felt conflicted, even guilty. You do what you have to do to help the people around you to be happy, but children are not supposed to bear the responsibility for their parents' happiness. That should not have been my burden, but I had definitely crossed that line and unwittingly taken on that role some time ago without even realizing it.

My father must have been suffering and he did break down a few more times — with me the day after she died, and again with the extended family after her funeral. These were short outbursts that, despite his attempts to quash them, suddenly jettisoned forth deep from his gut. It reminded me that I had only seen my father cry twice before this: the second time was when his mother died, a short outburst that seemed to take him completely by surprise; and the first was when I was in my teens.

I had accompanied Dad to the CNE, where he went to pay a visit to his client who owned a year-round restaurant on the fairgrounds called the High Noon. (Go figure!) Afterwards, we stopped briefly at an outdoor concert to hear a student choir sing "The Hills Are Alive" from *The Sound of Music*. It was beautiful and deeply moving, and as I looked over at my father, I was surprised to see him quietly crying, tears running down his cheeks. He just smiled at me without brushing them away. I never imagined my father had deeper sentiments than the ones I was used to — the swing between his morning highs and his more erratic and irritable lows. I was struck that I didn't know how to comfort him.

*   *   *

Bill and I got to work quickly, helping Dad adapt to life as a widower. I purchased a condo for him in the same neighbourhood he was used to, which I felt would help Dad adjust, especially in those first few months. "Do you think Dad will drink himself to death in the first year?" I asked my brother, remembering another one of his old war buddies who had done just that.

It was hard to imagine that anything had been tougher on Dad than losing his Cilla, but he showed us the survivor he really was. He immediately went to work adapting his life to this new reality — living alone after fifty-six years of marriage. I know he must have missed my mother terribly, but as with the war, he never talked about his pain — stiff upper lip and all that. He had always had a "let's get on with it" attitude, and, surprisingly, this was no different. In some ways I think he behaved as if he had finally been let out of the doghouse. Because, despite the way he treated her, Dad idolized my mother and had definitely felt more strongly about her than she did for him. My parents had many good times together, I reminded myself, but Dad further alienated my mother's affections with his frequent rages aimed at her.

In fact, my mother had told me that before my brother and I were born, she had contemplated leaving my father, alarmed by his drinking and wild temper. There was also another man, a friend of Billy's, Mom had said, someone rich and much older. But my mother had apparently given in when Dad found out, broke down, and pleaded with her to stay.

As a result, my mother ate her resentment a little at a time. Deep down she fumed. It was bottled up tight, but I knew it had festered inside of her, and without realizing it, I think my mother sank into a form of martyrdom — although it is hard not to feel that it was justified.

With this dynamic removed from his daily life, Dad seemed lighter and more focused. He embraced his independence almost like a new lease on life. I didn't know how to feel about this. I wanted my father to feel remorse for how he had treated my mother. I was probably really angry to see him doing so well. But on the other hand, I wanted him to be okay so that I wouldn't have to be the one to pick up the pieces of his broken life.

I jumped into action. I helped Dad arrange his move to the condo and set him up with all that he needed — a regular cleaning lady and Meals on Wheels, which brought an array of prepared meals to his door. He had never cooked anything more than a hard-boiled egg or a hot dog before (and watching him do that could be a harrowing experience).

Global Television had been wonderful to me during the weeks that I took care of my mother, continuing to pay my salary and extending their generosity until I was able to help Dad get organized. But then it was time to go back to work in Ottawa.

I, too, got on with it, believing I had done my mourning before my mother died. A few months after my mother's passing, however, I was having coffee with a colleague when for no apparent reason I burst into tears. The pent-up emotions of the past few months, the holding it all together for my mother while she deteriorated in those last weeks, spilled out. Mom and I had been each other's support, confidante, advisor, and ongoing coach. She was the person who had understood me best, and she wasn't there anymore.

With my mini-breakdown, my colleague injected tenderly, "And you are feeling that the wrong parent died." It was a journalist's blunt clarity.

It was alarming to hear someone say it out loud. It took me back to a night in my parents' kitchen when my mother was cleaning up after my father had gone to bed. He was drunk, as usual, and my mother was weeping over a full sink of dirty dishes. She rarely let her guard down. It was a really big deal when she did. She turned to me, and, with more exasperation than I had ever seen in her, she erupted, "Is it so wrong that I want him to die? That I want him to die so that I can have my own life?"

She and I both knew then that Dad was stronger than she was and that any hope of some peace in her life was empty. It pains me even to mention that I had secretly thought about that, imagining a day when my mother would be living on her own and doing exactly what she wanted every day. I knew it was never going to happen, but I admit I did think about it.

As she reached out and took my hands, she was finally admitting the bitterness that she had eaten all these years. In that moment I understood that I did not know what her dreams had been, what she had perhaps longed for and never realized, or the many ways her life had never been about her. I don't think my mother ever felt that she deserved her own life. That was the chasm between our respective generations. My mother did what was expected of her and made the necessary sacrifices to ensure that my life would be different, and it had been.

I was in equal measure grateful and filled with sorrow. I didn't know what to do that night, so all I said was, "I know, Mom, I know. I am so sorry. I am so very, very sorry." And she fell into my arms and just let go.

CHAPTER 19

JUST LIKE THAT

I fell into the role of dutiful daughter to my father as if it were the most natural thing in the world. Before my mother died I had maybe chatted with my father once or twice a month for a couple of minutes, but now I started checking in with him every day from Ottawa. I had never even done that with my mother. I guess I couldn't bear the thought of him being alone, and I guess I was also feeling lonely — my mother's passing had left such a big hole in both our lives. Dad was always so delighted to hear from me, and he started expecting my call. Maybe I was hoping to develop a deeper connection with him, so it just became a habit.

I have always had a sixth sense about what I am supposed to do next, even if I don't know what the implications will be or how it will all work out, and so it was with my decision to move back to Toronto. I was nearing fifty and, while I was grateful for the amazing career I had, I was restless. Billy had written somewhere that it sometimes drove him crazy to have so many things "buzzing around in his head." I felt that way, too. I had so many ideas I wanted to explore. I was done with telling news stories. Instead, I saw a market for helping people to tell their own stories. In fact, I had never met anyone who didn't have a great story to tell, and I felt I could do something with that.

The idea, I admit, was all very vague to start with, but as I worked on it, I realized that I wanted to go into business, and if I was going to do so, I needed to go where the money was — to the country's financial capital.

I did not intentionally move home again, but I followed my hunch that I was being drawn home for a reason.

On one of my trips to Toronto, I found and bought a house. Well, it was actually more complicated than that. One of my very best friends, Norman Sobel, was a real estate agent who also happened to be gay. By the way, my parents adored Norman. He was colourful and dramatic, all six feet, four inches of him, and he fit right into our wacky household. After my father first met Norman, he turned to me and said, "Now that's the kind of man you should marry!" And he wasn't kidding. I had to break it to Dad that Norman "played for the other team."

Anyway, Norman took me to see a house that he felt was underpriced in the current market, and after a tour we made a snap decision to buy it together. It was a crazy idea, and our friends quickly labelled us *Will and Grace* after the television show — but as I said, I was flying on pure instinct, and something told me it was the right thing to do.

A few months later, I left Global Television. And just like that, I found myself in the same city as my father, where I would end up front and centre, taking care of a man I believed had never really taken care of any of us, who had failed my mother as a husband and my brother and me as a father.

My brother, Bill, who was also living and working in Toronto, was a great help to me in establishing my new company, a communications business that I decided to call The Success Story Program™. And no, at the time I did not see the symmetry in the decision that played so conveniently into my family's narrative.

Both my brother and I had inherited an entrepreneurial spirit. We got that from Dad, for sure, and perhaps from Billy, despite his ups and downs in business. (My brother jokes that it might even go all the way back to Timothy Eaton himself.) As well, we had inherited the love of a story. For all his flaws, my father was a brilliant storyteller who knew how to both inform and entertain, whether it was with us at home, in his work, in front of a crowd, or in his wonderful books on Canadian military history. My father understood the power of stories and storytelling. The way I look at it now, stories are how our father gave love. It was the best way he knew how.

Dad's storytelling skills have had a profoundly positive impact on my life, although it took me some time to realize that. It is likely the reason I fell into journalism, a trade in which I could find and tell stories every day. But even more apparent to me now is what Dad taught me about the business of marketing stories. Living with a father who was always coming up with new ideas to promote and sell things, we were on fertile ground for conceptual discussions about how to package stuff to get people's attention. Dad initially fostered this talent in my brother and me, and it has served me well in all aspects of my life, as it would in my new endeavour.

My brother was very busy with his own business, and he had a family, so it was only logical that I would primarily be the one to watch over Dad. As was the case with most of my female contemporaries, this role often falls to the daughters.

My father had in no way prepared for his old age, either emotionally or financially. His business, while innovative and imaginative, never made the pot of gold he promised my mother. (My brother believes that Dad never charged enough for his services.) When he retired, he had few assets to speak of, neither property (he always rented, remember?) nor savings. It became clear to me as he adapted to the trials of getter older that he probably never thought he would. Dad just continued to live each and every day hoping it would all work out. Did that come from being born into a family of considerable means, or from being in the war, where he could not think ahead, where he expected that one day he might be shot down? I'm not sure.

Bill and I shared my father's condo expenses, and I don't know what we would have done without Veterans Affairs, because as a veteran, Dad was eligible for various independent living and health subsidies, which, thankfully, supplemented his diminished income.

Now that I was back in Toronto, Dad and I continued to talk on the phone every day, and since I was only about fifteen minutes away, I would also go over to see him at least once or twice a week. Dad was still able to go to his tennis club to see his friends, and people did come to see him, but he really looked forward to my visits — regular weekly entertainment where I was his sole audience.

I can't say I didn't enjoy seeing him. On the one hand I considered it my duty, but on the other he could still make me laugh, just as he had done with my mother. Our time together was usually in the evening over cocktails. I could never drink the way my parents did, although I had had my share of alcohol as a young adult. These days, while Dad downed a couple of double Scotches, I nursed a glass of white wine. Dad talked, mostly about the next book or article he was working on. I listened.

Over the last decade, his career as a writer had been in full swing and, while writing was not exceptionally lucrative, he was prolific. Eight of the twelve books my father authored on Canada and other military history were published in the nineties.

Dad was naturally drawn to telling stories of Canadian military heroes. He'd written three volumes of biographies about selected Canadian war heroes in the air (including his father, naturally), on the battlefield, and at sea. Then came *The Splendid Hundred*, about Canadians who excelled in the Battle of Britain; *Our Best and Our Bravest: The Stories of Canada's Victoria Cross Winners*; *Canada's Glory: Battles That Forged a Nation*; *Salute: Canada's Great Military Leaders from Brock to Dextraze*; and *Destruction At Dawn*, the project about the Bodenplatt Raid that I had researched for him some twenty years earlier. It was hard not to be proud of him.

With the start of the new century, Dad was still at it but winding down little by little. In 2001 he chronicled remarkable deeds of Canadians who saw action in the Second World War in an edition called *Unsung Courage*. Then he completed his collection with his own autobiography in 2002, entitled *Winged Combat: My Story as a Spitfire Pilot in World War II*.

Dad still would not talk about the war, but he was comfortable writing about it; however, even in his autobiography, where you might expect him to channel deeper reflections, he glorified his time as a fighter pilot. Writing about the period before D-Day, the Allied invasion of Normandy that took place on June 6, 1944, Dad was glowing:

> Looking back, I realize that month leading up to the invasion was one of the most enjoyable of my life. Oh! To be in England now that spring was here. They were exciting days, some of them romantic and fun, albeit not without their tragic moments of comrades lost. But that was all part of the game. History is being made and we were very much a part of it. In my youthful eyes all seemed right with the world. I found it thrilling.[*]

---

[*] William Arthur Bishop, *Winged Combat: My Story as a Spitfire Pilot in World War II* (Toronto: Harper Perennial Canada, 2002), chapter 16.

It seemed fitting for him to write an autobiography, a bookend to the remarkable writing career that Dad had begun in the mid 1960s with the biography about his father (*The Courage of the Early Morning*). Writing his own story brought it all full circle. Dad had wanted to call his autobiography *Winging It My Way*, playing on the Frank Sinatra tune, but his publisher decided on *Winged Combat*, playing on Billy's autobiography, *Winged Warfare* — as if any potential reader would ever make that connection. I considered this decision a missed PR opportunity and Dad agreed.

Every time Dad completed one of his books, he would give me a signed copy with an inscription on the inside page, such as, "To my lovely Pookie [he still called me by this nickname], from her loving Dad."

That always tugged at my heartstrings and forced me admit two things: one, how ashamed I was of the clash between my animosity toward my father and how much I loved him; and two, although I proudly displayed his ever-growing repertoire prominently on a bookshelf in my house, at that point I had only read two of his books all the way through — his biography about Billy and his autobiography. I really can't tell you why. Maybe I thought I would get around to it eventually, or maybe it was a silent protest.

*   *   *

It is difficult for me to pinpoint exactly when I started to notice the changes in my father. They crept up on me like a pot of tepid water slowly coming to a boil. Especially when you have an eccentric parent, it's hard to know when they begin to cross the next line.

For instance, Dad had always been absentminded about daily tasks, but now that my mother wasn't around to watch him, I had to be the one to remind him not to leave the tap running, and he would still do so. A number of times I came over to find him frantically mopping up the kitchen floor. Or once or twice he boiled an egg but then forgot to turn off the element on the stove, and I would always think how lucky it was that we discovered it in time. On another occasion, I arrived to find my father tending to a gash on his forehead. He had gotten a shock trying to change a light bulb and hit his head falling off the stepladder.

In his eighties now, Dad was also growing weaker. When he became unsteady on his feet, as older people eventually do, he got a walker. My father had an uncanny ability to embrace a new challenge, even disheartening ones like losing his wife or his motor skills, and still make the best of things. With his walker, he would charge up the street as he had always done. He'd pick up some groceries, stop for coffee, and churn his way back to the condo. He'd delight in telling me about the homeless man at the corner and his creative approach to begging for money.

"I got to give the guy credit," Dad said. "He calls out to people going past with things like 'I could get really excited about a sandwich!'"

Hearing it once was cute, but Dad quickly got fed up.

One day while the man held out his hand for some money and he called out to Dad, "Change, please!" My father barked back at him: "Please CHANGE!"

It was a little bit of daily theatre that satiated my father's need to keep the boring and mundane at bay. I had to admire him. He was awfully good at that.

Increasingly, however, Dad was also growing more agitated. His nerves had always been bad from both the war and the years of drinking, but now the little tasks were arduous. Even putting on his socks, he'd swear and curse, and his hands would shake, making it harder.

Dad spent a big part of his day in front of his computer writing, but that was becoming a nightmare, too. As for many of his generation, technology was a challenge, and learning the basics of word processing was gruelling enough, but now he couldn't type as well as he once had. He could never remember where his documents were or how to retrieve them. When anyone tried to coach him, well, there was an elevated chorus of cursing and swearing.

His telephone calls to me began to escalate, sometimes to two or three a day. He would start every conversation with "Hi, Pooks, have I got a problem!"

His telephone was apparently not working properly. "Do you hear that clicking in the background? It's driving me around the bend."

"No, there is nothing on my end," I would reply, and I really couldn't hear anything.

Or — "They are banging upstairs and my problem is I can't get any fucking work done!" he would shout.

Dad had always had relatively good health. Over the years he'd experienced stomach problems and developed an ulcer (the multiple Scotches were the culprit), and as ever — remember Harry the bird? — Dad believed more was better. He popped heartburn medication like candy and preventively took a couple of headache pills every night to ward off a hangover. By coincidence, his family doctor had an office right across the street. At first Dad respected the parameters of a check-up every few months, but then he started dropping by the office with his walker just to say hello — once a week, then two or three times a week. He wasn't sick or anything. I think he was just looking for a caring audience. I found that out because he kept talking about his doctor, with whom he was, by then, on a first name basis.

"Elizabeth checked my blood pressure again today," Dad informed me. "It was up a little more than yesterday," he added cheerily. When I questioned the doctor about his frequent visits, she was gracious. "It is a honour to take care of your father, and he certainly livens things up around here."

Dad was still drinking in those days, but less. He couldn't hold his liquor like he once had and was now easily appeased by a couple of stiff ones to reach the desired level of inebriation; and oh, yes, that bottle of Dewar's Scotch was still prominent on the kitchen counter next to the same old metal jigger that he had always used, now tarnished.

However, one day when I came over in the evening and poured myself a glass of wine, I noticed the bottle was gone and Dad did not have a drink in his hand. *Wait a minute.* It was after 5:00 p.m. *What gives?*

"Dad, you are not having a drink? You okay?" I asked.

"Yeah, sure," he said. "I quit."

"What?" I exclaimed, thinking that it was probably only temporary.

"Elizabeth says with the diabetes, I shouldn't drink anymore." Dad smiled.

As it turned out, he had only recently developed type 2 diabetes, and his sugar levels were still low enough not to require medication. Still, it was as if a freight train had smashed through the wall and flattened me. My father had stopped drinking? Just like that?

I should have been happy, but instead I was transported back to that painful revelation I'd had many years before when I considered that question — if Dad had to make a choice between the bottle and his family, what would he choose? I felt certain at that time that he would have picked the bottle. Now Dad had quit drinking because his doctor told him to? Not because I wanted him to or my mother wanted him to, but because it might harm his health … at eighty-five? I, myself, plan to START drinking heavily at that age! I had to sit down and take a long gulp of my wine.

What was even more infuriating was that Dad didn't seem to miss it. He quit cold turkey and never looked back, although, it didn't change much. I actually think quitting drinking just added to his chronic anxiety.

Then there was the trip to the hernia clinic.

Dad needed an operation to pop a piece of his intestine back into his lower abdomen. The recovery time was three days, during which someone had to stay at the clinic with my father. He had nowhere else to turn, so, of course, I was on deck.

I was waiting for Dad when they wheeled him out of the operating room. "Your father was very cross with us," the doctor said with some exasperation, before softening a little. "Must be the drugs. But he should sleep well now." The doctor left me with strict orders to make sure Dad stayed in bed for at least four hours.

Easier said than done.

I had already struggled with Dad the night before, helping him have a shower as we were instructed to do before his surgery in the morning. Dad had been so unsteady on his feet that I'd had to get into the shower fully clothed beside my naked father to hold him up while he soaped down — a father-daughter visual that I tried to block out immediately after.

The other patients on the floor who had all just had the same procedure were out cold. But within minutes of arriving back in his room after the surgery, my father, the oldest patient in the wing, was fighting to get up.

"Dad, please, you have to stop trying to get out of bed!"

"I have to go to the bathroom," my father said, despite being still drugged up from the anaesthetic.

I might have called for a nurse, but this was a private clinic where they provided the essentials — the operation, a nice room, meals, and an occasional check-in, but no extras like one-on-one nursing care. The staff had provided us with a blue plastic bottle with a wide mouth to insert you know what.

I had never actually seen my father's "you know what" before, and I was not about to look now.

Like most men, he had always been quite proud of it — joking with me that when he died he wanted an open casket. "Open from the waist down —" And he would smirk. "So all the women can see what they missed."

Ha! Ha!

Why had I never noticed before that Dad talked to me like I was just another of his fighter pilots buddies?

"Dad, you have to pee in this bottle because you are not getting out of bed."

"I can't do it."

"You can," I said calmly.

My poor father, following orders, sat partway up, fumbling for his willy as I brought the bottle up to it, averting my eyes, and then told him to pee.

I imagined all the people I had ever wanted to impress in my life seeing me at that moment and thinking, my goodness, she has certainly done well for herself — single, never married, given up a successful career as a TV news correspondent and filmmaker to try something completely new in her fifties. And in the last five years relegated to prime caregiver for one of the most stubborn and difficult fathers on the face of the earth, who is currently holding out his willy. (When I related this episode to my brother he roared with laughter.)

My father never did pee into that bottle. He didn't really have to, he just thought he did. Afterwards, as I pretended to empty the contents into the toilet so that he would settle down, my father did lie down and fall asleep — for half an hour. He was so agitated that he couldn't sleep, and getting through the nights with him was torture. Those three days felt like a life sentence.

In fact, it got so bad that two nights in I bolted. That's right, I got up and left. I took my car, drove home, and had a shower. I thought I might get back to work — when the phone rang.

"Is this Miss Bishop?" It was an administrator at the hernia clinic. "Are you coming back?" the woman asked.

"No, I hadn't planned to," I said quite honestly.

"I am afraid you can't leave your father here on his own." *So get your butt back up here* was the stern but silent message.

So I did. I got back in my car, drove up to the clinic, and pretended I had just gone out for coffee.

It was a wake-up call. I knew then that we had reached a need for the next level of care for my father. In the hopes of keeping him at home as long as possible, I arranged caregivers to come in and spend some time with him, helping him dress, bathe, and do the dishes.

Dad was still fearless, venturing out on his own with his walker, but sometimes I would get calls from the hospital that he had fallen down somewhere. Once he'd fallen in the middle of the street and had to be rushed to emergency. I would race to the hospital and find him in the hallway, lying rather pathetically on a stretcher. Fortunately unhurt, he would give me a sad look and tell me how sorry he was to make me come all the way down there. But he didn't look sorry, just really happy to see me.

As a result, I was encouraged to install a medical alert system. With a push of the button, Dad could summon an ambulance in an emergency.

That gave me a short respite from worry until my father decided that an emergency was a toothache, a sore neck, or a cramp in his leg. Dad pushed that button three times and three times the ambulance came to take him to the hospital with sirens blazing — all within a month or two. When he cried wolf that third time, I didn't even go to the hospital to see him, instead dealing with the situation over the phone. It was the right thing to do, but it didn't make feel any less guilty.

"Send him home, please," I said to the doctor, and they did, driving him back in another ambulance.

He wouldn't be home for long, though. It had been eight years since my mother had died, and it was one of the hardest things I ever had to do, but I knew my father couldn't live on his own anymore. He needed constant supervision and professional care. As anyone who has been through this with an elderly parent will tell you, the worst part is when you have to be the one to make that call.

CHAPTER 20

IT'S THE NURSING HOME FOR ARTHUR

It was early 2009 when my brother and I had the tough conversation with Dad about his next steps. The discussion was as awkward as we expected it would be, but I was so glad to have my brother there. Dad tended to be very businesslike when Bill was around, and he accepted his fate without a fuss in my brother's presence. I knew that Dad was probably in denial. I don't think he ever expected that things would turn out like this for the son of Billy Bishop. How much easier it was to die in your sleep at sixty-two than to face real old age and the dreaded decrepitude that can follow. That in itself takes courage.

Dad left it to me to scout out the alternatives for new living arrangements, but really, we knew, there was only one. Neither a retirement home nor an assisted-living facility were realistic options because they required resources that Dad didn't have. As well, at this stage, Dad needed full-time caregivers along with some nursing care that these living arrangements did not provide. Secretly, I think Dad was hoping to move in with me. I may have been a devoted daughter, but I wasn't crazy. It would be the nursing home for Arthur.

The City of Toronto provides a number of publicly funded nursing home facilities, and despite the negative overtones that one attributes to these types of institutions, the places I visited and staff I talked to were a delightful surprise. In a nursing home, Dad would also be eligible for monthly subsidies from Veterans Affairs to pay for his accommodation. I couldn't have been more grateful.

I quietly went through the process of putting Dad on a list for three nursing homes that I had approved upon inspection. Dad showed no interest in seeing them beforehand. He just expected me to take care of it and told me that he trusted my judgment.

We were warned that it would take about a year for a room to become available, and I thought that would give me the time to explain it all to Dad and for him to absorb the shock of his extraordinary life coming to this; but just three weeks later, we got the call. I was in Boston giving a seminar when Dad was notified that he had forty-eight hours to move into Kensington Gardens — a modern, bright, and sunny facility just north of the city's old Chinatown, and with highly dedicated staff.

Forty-eight hours is all we had to make one of the most emotionally charged, heart-wrenching transitions — moving a parent to a place where people go in but never come out.

We didn't have that conversation, of course. We scrambled to pack some clothes and a few personal items as I joked with Dad that finally he would have those "hot and cold chambermaids" his father had promised him. On arrival at the nursing home, I suppressed a chuckle when I saw the diverse, mostly female staff that had assembled, smiling brightly, to welcome my father.

He clearly enjoyed all the attention. He had a new audience, so he got through those first few days by behaving as though he were on a great new adventure — reminding me once again of his capacity to buck up and suppress his real feelings.

While I, too, was trying hard to keep my feelings of sadness at bay, I was relieved that Dad was now safe. He would have twenty-four-hour supervision and more than just me to be responsible for him. At the very least it felt like a reprieve.

For the first little while Dad did make the best of things, exerting his independence and pretending he was living in a hotel. He went out with his walker every morning after breakfast to get the newspaper at the corner store, as he had done at home, but he would get very annoyed when a staff member stopped him on his way out, asking where he was going.

"I can come and go as I please, right?" he demanded of me on our next phone call, to which I responded, "Of course, sure you can. They probably just like to know where you are going, just in case."

"In case of what?" he asked crossly. I quickly changed the subject, knowing I would feel the same way.

Except for meals, Dad refused to take part in any of the home's activities, such as group exercise classes, book clubs, or movie nights, because he didn't want to be bothered. Dad had never been a joiner. We installed a computer and printer in his room so that he could continue to do some work, and Dad kept a sign on his door that he never took down that screamed in big letters, "I am writing a book! DO NOT disturb." Translation: *Don't think that I am like the rest of you! I am important and I still have a life!*

Oh, the drama.

Around this time, the city of Toronto decided to rename its waterfront island airport after my grandfather — thankfully, the controversy was now well behind us. Formerly called the Toronto Island Airport, it was to be renamed Billy Bishop Airport. Its importance and prominence as a travel hub for the city was growing, so this was a great tribute to Dad's father and an honour for our family. Thereafter there would be two airports named after my grandfather in the province of Ontario, the other in Owen Sound.

My father was invited by the Toronto Port Authority to be an honoured guest at the opening of the new terminal, an event at which he would be treated like royalty. The nursing home staff, informed of who he was, helped Dad prepare and dress for the limousine that arrived at the door to chauffeur him downtown — probably a first for any nursing home resident.

To see my father in front of a large audience was to realize how frail he had become. As my brother helped him to the podium, Dad appeared confused, searching for his words; but then he relaxed and began to regale the large crowd of dignitaries — corporate executives, senior politicians, and media — with stories about how he and his father had enjoyed flying out of the island airport.

"My father loved to fly down low over a crowd of people and scare the shit out of them," he said provocatively.

In this new era of political correctness, the audience twittered uncomfortably while the press looked as if a fresh gale had flown into the terminal — Dad was indeed the last of a breed of "real characters."

Back at the nursing home they were all agog when Dad's picture appeared in the newspaper the next day, twittering that they had a celebrity in their midst.

Of course, Dad enjoyed having a fuss made over him. He got along well with the staff, but he had always bonded well with his caregivers. On the other hand, Dad was vociferously unimpressed with most of the residents, whom he liked to call "the other inmates," his real feelings about being in the home finally starting to come out.

"I have nothing in common with these people," he said. "Most of them have a case of the stupids." I have to admit, like my mother, I laughed sometimes when Dad was being outrageous.

To amuse himself and the staff, Dad gave some of them unflattering names. A Chinese gentleman in his nineties, a prince of a man, a former university professor who did the most beautiful calligraphy, Dad called "Cough Drop" because of his rather persistent cough.

Another woman, also ninety-something, sat across from Dad in the dining room. He called her "Awful Annie" because she scowled at his antics. "Old man," Awful Annie screeched at Dad one day, "You have no manners!" Good attention, bad attention — either way Dad loved it, and he taunted her regularly by sticking out his tongue or calling her an old bat.

There was also Mrs. Resendes, a lovely Portuguese lady whose room was across the hall from Dad's. She always smiled and waved at my father, while he complained constantly that she played her TV too loudly.

Several months later, I was at home when I got a phone call.

"Miss Bishop?"

"Yes?" I replied, and then seeing it was Dad's nursing home calling, "Oh, dear, what has he done?" I braced myself.

"Well, everything is okay, but there has been a small incident with your father," the nurse on duty announced.

Apparently, in the middle of the night, Dad had wandered over to Mrs. Resendes's room, unattended and unannounced, in nothing but his birthday suit to stand by her bed. Dad was disoriented, it seems, and Mrs. Resendes, apparently calm, got out of bed in her nightgown, pulled over a chair, and asked my father to sit in it — which he did.

"Then what happened?" I asked, incredulous.

"Well, the woman is rather religious, as you might be aware, and anyway, she got out her rosary and she put it around your father's neck."

Silence on the line as I tried to absorb how my father might react to this unexpected development.

"A rosary?"

"Yes … then she told him, 'God will help you, Mr. Bishop.'"

Dad had been baptized an Anglican but had never been a regular churchgoer, although I know he believed in God. He believed God got him through the war, he once told me.

Mrs. Resendes had then called for the night nurse, who found Dad still sitting in the chair, in the buff, with the Roman Catholic sacramental around his neck and coaxed him back to bed.

I didn't know whether to laugh or cry. The Arthur I knew might have done such a thing as a prank, but this was a new Arthur — not the one who had burnt so brightly in his own inimitable way, but a father that I couldn't yet quite grasp or accept, the one whose light was now beginning to dim.

Sometime before that, I am not sure when, people had started using the word *dementia* to describe my father's deteriorating mental state — in fact, they believed that Dad was having tiny mini-strokes. The paths in his brain were being short-circuited a little at a time, and no one was ever sure when they started or when they started to change things. There was, once again, no clear line. The changes snuck up on all of us.

It is always in the little things. Dad would ask the same question two or three times and demand the same answer over and over. His hearing was going and he refused to wear hearing aids, so I would have to repeat things multiple times. It frustrated him to no end, but then just about everything did.

Within about a year of being in the nursing home, Dad began asking what day it was. "Is it Monday or Tuesday?" he'd say.

"Tuesday."

"What happened to Monday? What did I do yesterday?" he would ask.

I didn't pay much attention. Hell, sometimes I forgot what I had done the day before. Some time passed, though, and then I noticed he couldn't tell me what month or what time of year it was, and in due course, Dad was not able to tell time at all. He stopped wearing his watch, and the big clock I had put up in his room didn't make sense to him anymore. Eventually, time just didn't mean anything to him. He would get up at all hours of the night and wander the halls ready for breakfast, as he had done that night before Remembrance Day.

As well, Dad's anxiety and anger mounted — he would get not just angry, but furious that the vents were blowing air onto his head while he slept. We fixed that by taping them up. But then he complained for weeks that he was too cold. We put in a space heater.

Then there was the mysterious itch. It was months before I could figure out what to do about that. One day, the moment I arrived for a visit, Dad pulled up his pant legs to show me where he had been scratching.

"It is driving me crazy! Crazy! Do you get it?" he shouted. I couldn't see any rash and I wondered if when some senses start to fade, others are accentuated. To try to placate him, I suggested an over-the-counter medicated cream. That appeared to soothe him for a week, but then he told me the itch was worse than ever and he couldn't wear socks anymore. The doctor prescribed a better cream. A week later Dad claimed the itch had spread up his arms.

It was one thing after another. He said his feet were swollen and so I went out and bought comfortable slip-on shoes for him. Dad was constantly getting terrible pains in his teeth. I arranged for multiple trips to the dentist. In fact, if he could find a problem where he needed to go for tests outside of the nursing home, he would find it. I finally clued in that he was just looking for an escape.

But on it went. Dad had a throbbing in his neck that was making him tired, then a cramp in his leg keeping him from a good night's sleep. If you touched the affected area to assess the situation, Dad screamed bloody murder.

No one was sure whether Dad's complaints were real or all in his head. Along with the nursing home staff, I tried to do what I had done all my life — satisfy my father's concerns one by one as they came up. In the case of the mysterious itching, which went on for months, we stopped using the nursing home laundry service, and I started coming in to do his laundry separately using non-allergenic soap. However, it didn't matter what I did, Dad found something else to keep me busy.

He had few visitors as he had outlived most of his contemporaries, but I can't say enough about a family friend, Jocelyn Minton, whom I eventually engaged to visit Dad several times a week. Dad became so attached to her that he started telling everyone they were getting married. "Where should we go on our honeymoon?" he asked each time she came for a visit. With great patience, Jocelyn deflected the conversation without deflating his hopes.

"How about you just figure out where you are going to get the money for our big wedding, Arthur."

When he was acting up, Jocelyn would give it right back to him. "If you think I am going to marry you behaving like that, you have got another thing coming, mister!"

Dad loved it and it settled him down for a bit.

For every cross word or unreasonable request Dad made, Jocelyn and the nursing home staff had a soothing word and astounding good nature. I marvelled at their infinite patience with my father because I was not doing as well. Even with all the staff's help, I felt that Dad was running me ragged. In addition to my increased visits to the nursing home, he was ambushing me with phone calls. He called me every day, and then as the dementia progressed, he'd forget that he had called me and call again, and then again and again. At one point he was up to eight to ten calls a day. At the beginning of this deluge, I answered them because you always wonder if something is really wrong. But hearing the phone ring and seeing "Dad" come up on call display all day long was taking its toll on me, and his messages were always disturbing.

"Jesus fucking Christ, I can't figure out this goddamn phone. Pookie, are you there?" or "Where are you? Why can't I find you? You are the only one that can help me with this. Oh for Christ's sake," and then you'd hear him trying to slam down the phone.

When I did answer the phone, my father sounded desperate and paranoid. I would run over to see what I could do. People were stealing from him, he claimed — taking his pens, his notebooks, and his wallet. Of course, I would locate these items easily in his drawer or behind his dresser, but this only pacified him for a little while.

Dad stopped watching television or listening to the radio, things that might have kept him occupied and distracted, and he slept fitfully, often having nightmares. One of his most disturbing was about a reunion of the guys in his squadron from the war. "It was so great to see them all — Hammy, Bitsy, Tex, Klersy, they were all there! But then — we were going somewhere in a bus and I don't know what happened. It crashed or something. Everyone was dead — dead! They were all dead. It was terrible."

Dad was actually shaking. I had never seen him let down his defences in relation to anything about the war. I had to take a step back.

There had always been other names for it — combat or battle fatigue; shell shock — but certainly the World War vets that I had met steered clear of ever talking about these conditions because, to their generations, there was such shame associated with them. Showing vulnerability related to the war was tantamount to being "yellow" or a coward.

But it was around this time that awareness of post-traumatic stress disorder was gaining prominence in both the public and the military. PTSD was being exposed; it was a real anxiety and stress disorder, and it required acceptance and treatment. This shift helped me to begin putting two and two together.

My father would never have been caught dead in a psychiatrist's office, so he had never been diagnosed. But I had watched Dad my whole life, and he had definitely exhibited many of the symptoms of PTSD — the permanent state of agitation, the hyper arousal, and the emotional numbing and avoidance of his personal experience of war. He had also been a fitful sleeper, and while he was old now and less in control of his emotions, how did I know that he hadn't always had these nightmares or flashbacks and had just kept them to himself? How did I know that my Grandfather Billy hadn't as well? Wasn't it likely that the glass of Scotch in my grandfather's bedside drawer had something to do with that? How did anyone survive over a hundred missions, facing unsure outcomes every time, without suffering from PTSD? I think many of them did, but nobody ever talked about it.

Before long Dad's ability to get around in his walker diminished and we moved him into a wheelchair. With that development, his demands and bad humour amplified. Since he could no longer get in and out of bed without help, he needed someone to take him to the bathroom. As if we all didn't have enough to do, Dad had also developed an obsessive need to pee every half-hour. His prostate was getting on in age, too, so even while he didn't really have to go, he felt the urge, and he wailed loudly when we told him to wait. He wailed even louder when we did take him to the toilet, accusing us of hurting him. There were some messy moments, which I'd just rather forget, as my father's dignity dissolved. I know so many in my generation who have or will have similar experiences as their parents age; as with everything, you don't know what you are up against until it is your mother or father.

Dementia is so terribly sad, especially if you worry your parent might have it for a very long time.

"How is his heart?" I would ask the doctor.

"Strong as a thirty-year-old," he'd reply.

"And his liver, despite all those years of drinking?"

"No worse for wear."

That I could not believe, but the doctor was probably trying to say that it wouldn't be his liver that would take my father down. I don't know if I was more depressed that Dad might suffer for too long or that I would.

You sometimes don't realize where your breaking point is. I had always been a lot tougher than I looked. My father used to say "as tough as three-inch steak," whatever that meant, and I seemed to have an almost unlimited well of tolerance and patience. The more Dad railed against my efforts, the more I pushed myself to beat him at his own game. I would get an instant hit of satisfaction when I was able to solve something for him. He would thank me, and I felt good, in control, as though everything were fine and in its place. A day later Dad would have a new problem, and I would despair and become anxious, wondering if what I did for him would ever be enough. And then I would get a second wind. I'd muster up my strength and tackle that problem, too, repeating this exhausting cycle.

"Poor man," people would say. "It's the dementia." I wanted to punch the wall whenever I heard that. I knew it was true, but at the same time it felt like others were making excuses for him. On some level, my father had always been like this — demanding, domineering, selfish, and ill tempered — and it felt all too familiar. When I lived at home with my parents so many years earlier, I had watched my mother become emotionally depleted by Dad's unquenchable neediness. My mother's anger had chafed and gnawed. Now it was happening to me; I had that feeling of being cornered. I was emotionally exhausted.

One day a nursing home staffer who knew our family, watching Dad's increasingly insatiable nature, blurted out the obvious. "Do you think your grandfather was so famous that your father never got the attention he needed and so he never felt good enough?"

I nodded, I think, but inside my head I was rolling my eyes. I was so tired of that excuse. Then two things happened that inadvertently tipped me over the edge.

The first came from Shardie, who had a talent for getting me out of my head and giving me a reality check.

"God help the people of the nursing home!" Shardie had laughed when she first heard Dad had been admitted to Kensington Gardens.

Shardie came with me to the nursing home a couple of times, calling Dad "the incredible shrinking man" as, with each visit, Dad had lost more weight and his dementia had progressed. "It's as if Arthur's body is getting smaller, but his personality [and she meant the negatives aspects of his personality, I think] is getting larger."

Shardie saw that I was slowly being beaten down, and she decided to join me at the nursing home again one afternoon after work. We spent about an hour with Dad, who was being difficult and insisting that he needed to go to the bathroom when he had just been five minutes before. As I saw it, he was getting more aggressive and unreasonable. What I didn't expect to hear from my best friend was a rebuke of my behaviour.

"Diana, this might come as a shock to you, but you are treating your father badly. In fact, you were being nasty and I have never ever seen you nasty."

"What do you mean? I have been taking care of him, giving my all to make him happy," I snapped.

"Yes, and I can see that you are at the end of your rope," Shardie continued. "But you were verbally and physically aggressive with your father back there, barking at him and almost manhandling him when he was trying to get up and you were trying to get him back in bed."

"Oh, God," I said, as I tried to take this in. I was expecting my best friend to acknowledge my victimization, not challenge my role in it. But I knew that Shardie was my barometer when life threw a curve ball. She had always been able to bring clarity to my confusion and help me to see things as they really are. Was I becoming like those TV commercials I had seen recently of family members abusing their elderly senile relatives — pushing around or even stealing from their parent or grandparent? I could now see how it could happen. Just as I had been unable to notice the subtle changes in my father from one day to the next, I had not seen them in myself either. It was hard to accept and humbling to realize how unaware I was. I never liked being exposed for being human, when I think about it — or for not being the perfect daughter, the person that I had strived so hard to be. How wearing it all was — this lifelong habit.

That was definitely a low point.

The second thing that jarred me into a new awareness came from my brother. Bill's relationship with his Dad deserves a book of its own, and I will not be the one to tell his story, but I can say he made the choices he needed in order to take care of himself while still providing what emotional support he could to me. The trouble was that I was often too proud to ask for his help. But I know he was worried about me, and one day he called. "Dad doesn't treat me the same way as he treats you," my brother proclaimed. "He expects you to take care of him like Mom did. He can't get away with that with me." And then Bill gave me the following option. "Here is what we can do. I will take Dad off your hands for ONE year. I will take over his care, his finances, whatever — all his needs, and give you some time to get your life back."

Wow, that sounded good, and I took a breath. But he wasn't finished. "But if I do this, I want you to promise me one thing — that you will walk away and you will not go and see Dad at all for one whole year. Do you think you can do that?"

It was a lot to take in. I was blindsided on so many levels, I didn't know how to react, so I didn't. I said I would think about it.

In the days that followed I felt physically sick. Was my brother actually saying that he would help with Dad? It was help that I could certainly use, as it had been such a lonely struggle until then, years of it — but not to go and see Dad for a full year? The choice made my head spin. It felt like a test. At the thought of not having to tend to Dad's almost daily physical and emotional demands and anxieties, yes, I could feel the relief, but that was followed by my own deep well of anxiety. Not see him? What would Dad do? Wouldn't he wonder where I had gone? Would he think that I had betrayed and abandoned him? And worse still, what if Dad died during that year and I had not been there for him? I would never get over the guilt.

If I accepted Bill's terms, I would be letting my father down. If I didn't, I would be letting my brother down by not doing what he thought was best for me. Trapped. Either way.

It had not been the best-conceived idea, and my brother later admitted as much, as he really just wanted to help me. But it did serve a purpose. I realized that even if Bill stepped in to attend to our father, my sense of responsibility to Dad would not end there. I had tried to satisfy my father's ravenous demands, almost as if, ultimately, I was trying to take away his pain of not feeling good enough. I thought I could fix him. I had always wanted to fix him.

But it was a battle I couldn't win, and my brother knew that. He was just trying to save me from turning into my mother.

CHAPTER 21

HUGGING THERAPY

I didn't take my brother up on his offer, but his input along with Shardie's had been a rude awakening.

It was so very hard to watch my father struggle with his demons and try unsuccessfully to outrun his emotions, unable to find peace within himself, especially at this stage in his life where he no longer had any control. Dad was on course to die angry. And I was on course to still be angry with him when he died.

Like my mother, I had suppressed my rage. I had developed almost a phobia about it. In my family, I had been led to believe that women did not get angry. They were supposed to take what was thrown at them and buck up. Fighting back only made things worse. As a result, I never learned how to express anger or deal with confrontation in any constructive way. Instead, I ran away from it, swallowed it whole, and trained myself not to feel it.

I was feeling my anger now. It was real. It was a big ball of red-hot fury in my chest that could no longer be tamed or held down. I would wake up in the middle of the night, get up, and walk around, wondering what to do with it, how to get it out, how to make it dissolve. It had always made me very tired, made me want to sleep. Now it was keeping me awake. I couldn't hide anymore. I imagined myself running out into the night screaming my head off, but I knew I couldn't do that, so I pounded the bed trying to release it. I pounded harder and harder, my arms like live wires spurting an electric charge down and out through my fists. As long as I could keep it up, I would pound the bed; when I was drained, I'd crunch up in the fetal position sobbing. It felt so undignified, but I didn't care. I had kept it locked up for too long.

Allowing myself to feel was a big step because the more I let go with my anger and frustration, the more I understood it, and the less power it had over me. I decided to just keep pounding the pillows — because it was working. Perhaps I could not keep my father from leaving this world an angry man, but I could change my anger and resentment toward him. To do that I knew I needed to be patient with myself and with my father. I felt that I needed to become more of an observer than a participant, to notice things that I had not paid attention to or given any significance to before — and while I waited for something to reveal itself, I kept pounding.

Following one of his trips to the nursing home, my brother pointed something out. "Do you see what has happened to Dad's right hand?"

I knew that it had tightened up, the fingers cramped into a semicircle where the tendons had calcified with age. Dad had undergone one operation already to help straighten them out, but then it just happened again.

"It's as if he is still holding that glass of Scotch," Bill hypothesized. He was right. My father is right-handed. For seventy years or more, Dad held a glass of Scotch in his right hand, imbibing that golden tonic more often than any other liquid.

However, Dad was no longer reaching out for that next drink. He didn't drink anymore. But he was still reaching out. I could placate him with a visit, fulfill his incessant demands, but still he would reach out again for more and more — of me.

I had become Dad's drink. But he had become mine, too. I didn't have a drinking problem, but I was also addicted — my addiction was trying to fix him. I did that by trying to fix everything he complained about. *Fix it, Diana. Then wait. You will have to fix something else, but keep fixing, and one day maybe it will stop. He will be fixed. Then you will have peace. Then you can relax. Then you can be happy.*

But it never worked for my mother, did it? Instead, she became resigned and bitter. I could not and would not let that happen to me.

Since Dad had been in the nursing home, I hadn't hugged him at all. As I have said, I never hugged him much, anyway. I had certainly seen my father reach out for it, just as he had always done with me, but I shirked it off. "Oh, Dad, don't be silly." I didn't want that closeness with him. I was wary of his mood swings and probably feared that I could be engulfed by his neediness and self-loathing. Sure, I gave him a cursory kiss on the cheek before I left, but I had become so automatic in my duties that I had stopped seeing Dad as a human being in need of love. He had become a chore to be tended to.

Then one day as he talked on about something, I turned off the sound of his voice in my head and really looked at him. I wondered, when was the last time anyone really hugged Dad? Not that kind of hug you get when you are greeted by someone, but one where you are scooped up in someone's arms, safe, secure, loved "beyond belief," as Dad might even say. Never had I seen Dad receive that kind of love from anyone.

My father, who never felt he measured up, probably didn't think he deserved love — because if he had felt loved, he probably would have behaved better. When Dad reached out, like he did for that drink, he was reaching out for love; but he did not really expect anyone to reach back, and his chronically inappropriate behaviour, which he used to get attention, was a means of self-preservation to ensure that nobody would.

Over several weeks I pondered reaching my arms out to him, only to feel myself flinch inside as I had always done. But now I noticed, felt, and paid attention to my innermost thoughts. If I gave him that hug, he would just want another and then another. It would never be enough. *When will it be enough?* I thought.

That's when I decided to hug him anyway. To do the thing that both frightened and repelled me. As insane as it seems, I needed to summon my courage even to attempt it.

The next time I arrived at the nursing home, I found my father in his room, lying in bed taking a nap. He woke with a start when he saw me and I said softly, "It's okay, Dad. It's just me." I took off my coat and took his hand as I sat on the side of his bed.

"Hi, Dad," I said. "I want a big hug. Can you do that, can you give me a big hug?"

This time it was Dad who seemed unsure, but after a moment's pause he reached out to me. I took a deep breath and lifted his diminishing frame so that I could wrap my arms around him and hold him tight. My father smelled faintly of a sick person, someone in need of a bath. I really didn't want to do it. It felt foreign, unnatural, but I kept saying to myself, *Just hug him, hug him. What harm can it do?*

My father began to tremble, his arms shaking more and more violently. For a second, I felt that he was going to repel the hug, as if he would not be able to accept the thing he craved most. It occurred to me then how very much alike we were. How long had it been since I had allowed anyone to hug me like that, to accept the love I craved?

We remained steadfast in our embrace.

"Don't let me go, Dad. I love you. I really do." And when I said it, for once I actually meant it.

"I love you too, Pookie," my father said meekly, and I knew he always had.

Every time I saw Dad from that day forward, I repeated this ritual. The more I did it, the easier it became, and the more I felt it was real and true. I even looked forward to it.

That's how I began to forgive my father. It wasn't a tap I turned where forgiveness suddenly spilled out in a gushing stream. Forgiveness is an invisible force that moves along incrementally, and you don't think you're making any progress until one day you find you have crossed the threshold to the other side. That day came when I was able to ask myself if I could just forgive Dad — despite all that had happened — if I could just love him — despite it all — or at least entertain the idea that I could.

And then I would hug him. And then hug him again.

Eventually those hugs reverberated into my past. They took me back to the day so many years before when that frightened little girl had stood outside the bathroom door after telling her dad he was drunk. I had been shocked when he yelled at me and told me to never say that to him again. Now I imagined someone wrapping that cowering child in a big hug and telling her she was honest, smart, and brave. I imagined that the person enveloping me in a loving embrace and giving me that unconditional hug was the grown-up me, and I felt her love so deeply.

Finally, I was safe.

CHAPTER 22

DAD'S WAR

In a surprisingly short period of time, after keeping up with my "hugging therapy," I noticed an emotional space that opened up between Dad and me. The resistance that had always felt like an electric fence repelling me when I got too close was diminishing. It is amazing what happens when you can just let go. Instead of anger, I was sending love Dad's way. There was a precious flow between us and, thankfully, still some time left to enjoy it.

That's not to say that Dad had turned into a little angel. Sadly, the dementia was progressing and he was becoming more aggressive and anxious. He made even more noise now. He howled that we were hurting him when we tried to get him dressed. He thought people were out to get him, and sometimes he didn't make a lot of sense.

When I arrived and gave him our special hug, I would ask, "How are you today, Dad?"

"Not too good," he'd reply. "I have been in a coma for a few days."

Things like that.

His short-term memory had all but disappeared. For almost two years we had exactly the same conversation over his favourite Saturday or Sunday lunch, a juicy hamburger — meat, no bun, a ton of french fries, and a mound of ketchup. Food was his biggest comfort now; at this stage I let him eat whatever he wanted. I patiently let Dad talk on and on about the book that, sadly, he would never write — another one dedicated to people who had proudly served our country. He'd had an idea for a coffee-table book of quotations from famous leaders in battle, or short anecdotes from his experiences during the war years. It gave Dad a focus and purpose, and he became obsessed with finding a title.

As he was more than a little bit confused about everything, I would volunteer some ideas. "How about *Canada's Proud Military Heritage in Punch Lines?*"

Dad would nod. "Yes, that's good. Write that down."

I would write it down for him. The next week he'd forget about it and we'd start all over again. We had that same conversation so many times that I felt like Bill Murray in the movie *Groundhog Day*, finding myself in a time loop repeating the same day over and over. In a way it was kind of sweet and funny, and a sense of humour is what keeps you sane during something like this.

Dad's long-term memory took longer to leave him, but when that started to happen, I knew that the window on any semblance of the father I once knew was closing. His recollections were waning. Dad could always be counted on to recall those amusing stories about his father, but at this point he talked about Billy less frequently, and when I prodded him to tell me one of his stories, Dad looked at me blankly as if he were trying to connect some long-lost series of dots.

I watched my father decline, and it dawned on me how much I would miss hearing him tell those stories, even the ones he had told so often that it used to make me roll my eyes. As my father liberally coated another french fry with ketchup, it struck me that I was watching history disappear. Not only was Dad one of the most knowledgeable chroniclers of Canadian military history, he was one of the few people left who actually knew Billy Bishop. On top of that, what I also tended to forget was that I was losing my father's own history. Dad's breed of Second World War fighter pilots were also fading away, and it further saddened me to think that I had never successfully gotten Dad to open up to me about his side of things: about his own war and what he had lived through.

Of course, he had not made it easy for me, even in his more lucid days. And I was now remembering a few things that had happened ten years earlier that hadn't really registered with me before this.

In 2002 when I made *A Hero to Me*, my father had accompanied me to the Billy Bishop Regional Airport in Owen Sound to celebrate the eighty-fifth anniversary of my grandfather's raid on the German aerodrome.

On display among the aircraft from both world wars was a vintage Spitfire, the plane my father flew. At the time I thought that this might be a good moment to talk to him about his own flying experience.

The Spitfire was a British-built aircraft, an engineering marvel of its time. It was a lot faster than the First World War machines, and the Spitfire had a similar cachet. Not only did it have an elegance all its own, but when you heard that Merlin engine, you couldn't mistake it for anything else. Even I got goosebumps seeing one fly past.

As Dad and I circled the plane together, the onlookers encouraged him, and my father climbed into the cockpit and regaled us with a story about how he had once crashed his Spitfire. I knew that, like his father, Dad had had a few mishaps, but I had never really heard him talk about them.

The incident occurred after a routine air test, he told us. As he was heading back to the field, flying at about one thousand feet, an explosion suddenly jolted his plane. Dad looked around and saw flames coming from the fuel tank. "The plane was shaking like mad and losing altitude rapidly, and I was too low to bail out," he explained. "Pieces of metal were flying off the aircraft and I was trying to hold the stick steady. That's when I saw two poplar trees dead ahead, and I thought *I am done for.* I shut my eyes, and everything went blank."

"What happened, Dad?" I volunteered, as a crowd leaned in around him.

"The next thing I knew I was sitting at the end of the airfield across the road — and looking behind me, I saw the Spitfire resting on its belly, flames licking the top of the engine hood."

"And you were okay?" I asked, incredulous.

"Yes, not a scratch or even a bruise," Dad said.

"How is that possible?" I went on.

"I dunno," Dad replied, looking as if he still couldn't believe it after all this time.

It was surprising that Dad survived the crash, but even more astounding to me was that I was finally hearing something that sounded authentic and unrehearsed from my father, albeit still without any deep insight into his feelings.

I got a rare glimpse of those when Dad and I were filmed paying a visit to Billy Bishop's grave in the family plot in Greenwood Cemetery just south of Owen Sound. I had been there a few times before, but never with my father.

The cemetery was large, and we didn't have a map, so it took us a while to locate the grave. I had quipped to Dad, "That would look good, eh, if we can't even find it?" We both chuckled.

Finally, we spotted the shiny grey tombstone with BISHOP emblazoned on it in black letters. The camera rolled. As the two of us wandered around, preoccupied with our own thoughts, my father suddenly stopped and put his hands on his hips. He looked at his father's name on the headstone with sudden reverence. A Canadian flag was planted next to the tombstone — a simple, poignant gesture. The ashes of this famous man rested here, a man I had never known but ultimately loved with every ounce of my being, and the man my father considered the biggest hero of them all.

"Give him the old salute," my father said softly as he brought his right arm horizontal, elbow bent and fingers pointing to his temple.

There it was. A tender moment — on the cusp of an honest, heartfelt private emotion — like my dad was remembering his dad and was suddenly lonely for him.

It was not something he ever would have admitted, but I saw it and the camera captured it.

I felt closer to him then, though I felt a momentary sense of loneliness, too. This could be me one day, here, looking at *my* father's grave.

Over the course of our filming back at the airport, I prodded Dad about his father, about what was it really like to be the son of Billy Bishop. How hard was it to have such a legend hanging over him as he went into a Second World War?

I was trying to find some crack in his psyche; instead I got the usual pat answers.

In frustration, I asked, "But you must get sick of people always talking about your father and not about you?"

He didn't deny it. "But you didn't get anywhere thinking like that," he said abruptly.

I was so discouraged that I let Craig, my director, do the main interview with my father for my documentary. Dad always seemed to relate better to a guy anyway, and was a little more forthcoming with him, though not much. I knew Dad would have dismissed some of my questions as he always did, but with Craig he revealed a hint of bitterness when talking about his father, which I hadn't noticed before.

"I wasn't worried about my old man at all," Dad almost growled. "He wasn't teaching me how to fly. He wasn't teaching me anything. I wasn't thinking about what people thought of him or me or anybody else."

Back at the nursing home all these years later, I reflected that I would never know more; I had lost my chance.

Then one day, we were just sitting eating lunch when I asked Dad a simple question. "What was it really like to fly a Spitfire, Dad?"

He paused, and I thought he might just give me one of his empty stares, but instead he said, "De Bub used to say ..." ("De Bub" was Bob Hayward, a member of Dad's squadron.) "De Bub said, 'You don't fly a Spitfire. You wear it like a glove and then you just wave it around.'" Waving his crippled former drinking hand to demonstrate, Dad repeated softly and slowly with such a sweet smile, "You just *waaaave* it around."

It gave me pause. I had seen a look of wonder and respect come over people's faces when they learned that Dad had flown Spitfires in the war. It was an auspicious detail about his life that had separated him from his father. A 1943 article that appeared in a Canadian newspaper when Dad was in the middle of his tour read: "Bishop's father ... shot down 72 enemy aircraft during his career in the last war in his famous Nieuport fighter — slow stuff beside the swift 'Spit' son Billy is flying."[*]

Yes, indeed. Some people called Dad "Billy" too in those days — one more thing to make it harder for him to come out from under his father's long shadow. But how my father must have secretly been thrilled by that comment.

I wish I could tell you that we had many more days like this, but we didn't. More often Dad didn't have an answer to my question, or he was off somewhere between here and gone.

I never stopped hugging him, though.

And that's when I decided I should start reading his books.

Very few of us who had parents and grandparents in the two world wars are lucky enough to have a written history of their stories. Not only do I have my grandfather's autobiography and biography (the latter written by my father) and my father's own autobiography, but I have all the other books that Dad wrote about the multitude of Canadians who distinguished themselves in battle. In fact, they have always been there, right in front of me.

They dominate several shelves in my bookcase at home, and I certainly enjoy it when people, rather astonished, inquire, "Wow! Did your father really write all of these books?"

"Yes," I answer.

Back then they assumed that I had read them all. I hadn't. Sure, I'd flipped through them over the years, but I hadn't been all that interested in

---

[*] Bishop, *Winged Combat*, 114.

the subject matter. I had also heard all about their contents in the evenings from the time that first drink was poured, and Dad would talk to either my mother or me or both of us about what he had written that day. It was as if I had already read them, anyway. My silent protest, as I said.

How ironic. Dad had kept his father's medals hidden away in his under-wear drawer. I kept Dad's books hidden away by not reading them. Perhaps I really was hiding — hiding from the magnificence of my own father's contributions.

Dad wrote because that was where he channelled his emotions. By not having read his books, I had cut myself off from what really made my father tick, from who he really was, from the empathy I might develop for him and that emotional bridge that might allow me to fully forgive him.

By personally and internally acknowledging the magnitude of his con-tribution to Canada's military history in those tomes of dedicated research, commitment, and allegiance — collections that are still in bookstores and libraries around the world — I would be admitting my father's powerful legacy — one of his own making and not his father's. And that would be admitting that Dad might be a hero, too.

I had been going about things all wrong. I had spent so much time asking Dad about what it was like to be Billy Bishop's son, questions that everyone always asked him, questions that he felt were his duty, even his life purpose, to answer. I hadn't thought to ask him about what he really cared about and wanted to talk about — such as what it was really like to fly a Spitfire. And what was your war like, Dad? And why did you dedicate your life to record-ing the heroic efforts of Canadians in wartime? Maybe I knew how he would answer those questions, but the point was that I never asked him. As a jour-nalist I had discovered that the simplest questions often elicit the most candid responses. How many of us don't ask our family members those questions because we take the answers for granted and assume we already know them?

Dad had few lucid moments left. He mostly talked gibberish. He invented stories that seemed real to him but sounded to the listener as if he had just woken up from a strange dream.

"I keep losing my wives," he told me one day.

"Oh, my, how many do you have?" I said, playing along.

"Sixty-eight, I think, but one of them disappeared in quicksand. I can't find her."

"Ah, well, I am sure she will turn up," I replied.

He looked satisfied with the remark.

Obviously, it was too late to ask him the questions that were coming to me as I read through his books — about Canadians on the battlefields in the South African Boer War, Dieppe, Antwerp, and Korea. My father had written about them all, and as I became engrossed in the details, I had to stop every so often to remind myself to hear the words on those pages in my father's voice — the father I used to know.

I had lots of questions now, and while my father could no longer answer them, I sat with him and imagined that he could. I was surprised by how much I had actually known but never appreciated.

"What was the most exciting time you ever had as a fighter pilot, Dad?" I asked in my imaginary conversation.

"D-Day," I think Dad would have replied, based on my rereading of his autobiography.

D-Day, of course. That was the day, June 6, 1944, when Dad's squadron, one of many, flew across the channel and patrolled the Normandy coast as cover for the British and the Canadian armies that made their way inland to crack the Nazi grip on Western Europe. I knew from my reading that, leading up to the invasion, Dad, age twenty-one at the time, was pumped to be at the centre of it all. History was being made.

"That was when you shot down the German aircraft, right?" I asked in my pretend conversation.

Remember Dad's joke — that between he and his father, they had shot down seventy-three German planes? Billy shot down seventy-two and Dad shot down one!

"Not that day. The next day, D-Day plus one," Dad replied in my imagination.

Dad had gone on the first patrol that day. With the success of the invasion the day before, the armies had advanced inland and Dad was flying back and forth over about a twenty-kilometre area, where the squadron was more likely to run into enemy aircraft, which they eventually did.

"There was a JU-88, a German bomber, that we caught in our sights," Dad would have told me. "We played hide and seek with it for a while through the cloud cover trying not to get shot at or crash into each other. Gradually the JU lost height and as I had it within range, at about four hundred yards, I took aim and let go a ten-second burst. The volley knocked the bomber's tail off. That's when the Junkers hit a fence and exploded into a ball of fire."

"What happened then?" I asked, entranced by my make-believe exchange.

"I hollered *Yahoo!* Like I just roped a steer," Dad said with enthusiasm. "Fortunately, nobody heard me — I hadn't flicked on the radio transmitter."

This was a direct quote from his autobiography, and I felt he probably wasn't being completely honest. I think Dad would have wished that someone had heard him.

"Scariest flight ever?" I asked my father as my virtual interview continued.

"Too many to name them," I knew he would probably say, as he was never shy about admitting he was afraid. Neither was Billy.

My father survived five accidents, including that one where he had crashed into the trees and woke up on the other side of the street. Like so many pilots of his day, I discovered that my father had skirted disaster many times in the hundred or more sorties that he had survived. A hundred or more! This was no game.

"When we flew, you had to focus, stay in formation, stay attuned to the performance of the aircraft," I know Dad would have said, "while keeping a sharp lookout for the enemy or that you didn't run into one of your own guys."

Dad had witnessed one of his closest friends bail out after battling engine trouble, tragically too low to use his parachute, only to be gobbled up by the cold English Channel water. I tried to imagine watching that happen to one of my friends. I couldn't. Dad had seen so many of his fellow pilots shot down, killed, or taken prisoner, and he had managed somehow to go on to fight another day.

"I had a dinner date at eight to think about, for Christ's sake!"

Yeah, I could hear him saying that, too, glamorizing it all.

It is clear, even in Dad's books, that he felt his purpose was to exalt his memories of war. He unabashedly praises and honours Canadians who served their country. I believe that my grandfather's and my father's generations viewed heroes, especially war heroes, very differently than we do now. Today the era of the iconic military war hero has all but evaporated as warfare has changed. My father knew that, and he wanted us to remember the best of them, and to be inspired by their courage and heroism.

In Dad's autobiography, there is one passage that comforts me because it feels like it came from a deep place in his heart, and because I know he really believed it — although, it seems so contrary to how subsequent generations view war now.

My father had been escorting an American bomber that had been damaged by flak. It was a beautiful summer's evening as they crossed the English Channel, and he wrote, "The sky was clear, and from 5,000 feet the sea was a deep azure blue, tranquil and calm. It was so serene and peaceful that I felt lucky to be alive, fortunate to be a fighter pilot as I reflected on the wonderful life we led."*

The wonderful life we led.

I can't imagine one of our fighter pilots returning from Syria or Iraq today, or a soldier coming home after a tour in Afghanistan, boasting publicly about the *wonderful life they led*. It's a testament to how the face of war has changed since my father's and grandfather's time.

I glanced at the tiny man sitting across from me nibbling at his lunch, seemingly content as he munched on another french fry, ketchup dripping down his chin, oblivious to our simulated chat. My dad had never been comfortable with the "hero" label. He preferred being called a "survivor." I hoped he could feel this new loving current flowing toward him from his only daughter, because for the first time in my life, I was bursting with pride. Yes, I was so very, very proud of my father.

---

* Bishop, *Winged Combat*, 147.

CHAPTER 23

Remembrance Day

The last Remembrance Day ceremony I ever attended with my father was at his nursing home on November 11, 2012. It was a much smaller affair than the public ones we were both used to and, having seen my father deteriorate so rapidly, it was for me, certainly, the most emotionally charged.

Just before the service started, the nursing home chaplain asked me to read Lieutenant-Colonel John McCrae's famous war poem, "In Flanders Fields." As a seasoned broadcaster, I had always been able to take on this duty with the appropriate veneration and control, and I thought it felt especially important for me to do so this time.

The nursing home had assembled a small group of residents and family members, some of whom were veterans of the World Wars and the Korean War. Now in an advanced stage of dementia, my father sat among them, a crumpled figure in a wheelchair.

The staff had been able to get him dressed in his blue suit, which was now miles too big for him. He had a red poppy on his left lapel and his medals beneath it. He wore sunglasses to protect his eyes from the glare of the overhead lights, which made him look rather fierce as he held with all his might, or it seemed, a determined look on his face. He was back fighting, fighting to hold on to life.

When the time came, I went up to the front and began the poem. I barely got through the first sentence —

"In Flanders fields the poppies blow

"Between the crosses, row on row ..."

Panic. It seized me as the images of the soldiers' graves became real. I had been able to keep a distance from these words many times before, but this day I was strangled with emotion. I couldn't take my next breath as I suppressed a sob that caught me unawares and I stumbled on the words.

"That ... that ... that mark our place —"

Then I stopped and couldn't go on.

"Take a moment," the chaplain whispered in my ear. I felt the room grow tense.

In those few seconds I looked over at my father, who I am not sure even knew it was me at the front doing the reading. He continued to look straight ahead, eyes shielded by the sunglasses, holding on for both of us.

My overwhelmed state gave me a new perspective on all Remembrance and Veterans Day ceremonies across the country and around the world, where people remember, with great respect, remember generations of family members who have fought on battlefields since the First World War.

I recovered a minute later and was able to finish reading the poem. "The torch; be yours to hold it high.

"If ye break faith with us who die

"We shall not sleep, though poppies grow

"In Flanders fields."

For the next three months, my father was in and out of the hospital with various infections. One night I arrived late in the evening to sit with him. The lights were off in his room, but he was awake, rocking himself back and forth, side to side, restless and unable to lie still.

A saving grace in what had been a long road for both of us was that Dad still recognized me. "Pookie — oh, thank goodness you are here," Dad said as he fidgeted with his hands and couldn't keep his legs still.

"I am here, Dad," I said, gingerly giving him our hug. He seemed so fragile; I was afraid to break him.

"Did you see him?" Dad asked as I gently released him.

"Who?"

"The Old Man," Dad said.

"Billy?" I asked, suppressing a smile.

"Yes, he's here and I am going off to have a drink with him soon."

"Scotch?" I mused.

"You bet, a double," Dad replied.

A wave of warmth came over me. I felt Billy there with us. I wanted so much to ask Dad, "Can I come with you, just for a little while?" because I would have given anything to see Dad and Billy together, to see for myself the chemistry between them, how similar they were, and also how different. I had a lifetime of feeling their strong presences and knew, even in death, they would always be with me.

Before I left, I did our little ritual that I had started whenever we parted.

"How do you fly a Spitfire, Dad?"

"You don't fly a Spitfire," he began, and then I joined him in unison. "You wear it like a glove and then just wave it around." We both waved a hand with a swoop.

Two days later, Dad was back in the nursing home on death watch. I was in the car heading back again to see him when my cellphone rang. It was the nurse on duty, and she asked me to pull over. I knew what she was about to tell me but, hoping I could still get there in time, I kept driving.

"I am so sorry, Diana, I know you are on your way, but your dad has just passed away."

The infection that had been coursing through Dad's body had finally claimed him and his heart had stopped. He had taken his last breath alone, but somehow I knew he would … and all I could think was *what a blessing*.

It was, coincidentally, February 14 — Valentine's Day — and my mother's and my favourite day of the year. "You little bugger," I said affectionately under my breath. "You die on the day dedicated to love — you really know how to get to me."

He had gotten to me. My father had been a difficult and narcissistic man all his life. He had been demanding in his need for attention, maddening in his inability to change, and brutish when things didn't go his way. But when my father was full of fun, there was no one more alive, and his energy could fill a room. I would miss that. I really would.

I did pull over then, and the dam in my heart burst. I sobbed. It is always a shock when someone dies even when you are expecting it. I was crying from the shock, but I was also releasing some of the tension of those last few years, and I felt the relief of knowing that it was now over.

The newspapers paid tribute to my father, but it was my brother who crafted the fulsome obituary. It began with a quote from American writer

John Updike that my father had also used at the beginning of his autobiography: "Being born of fame is not like earning it. You have to create your own worth in other coin; you have to escape history's shadow and get, as they say, a life."

The obituary continued:

> Family and friends are remembering and celebrating the life of Arthur Bishop, who passed away this week at the age of eighty-nine. Colourful, outspoken, hilarious, fearless, pugnacious, loquacious, prolific, and determined — Arthur Bishop was all of these things and more.
>
> Arthur's outrageous jokes, priceless stories and strong opinions will be long remembered by everyone who knew him ... He will also be fondly remembered by John Dewar & Sons for his single-handed strengthening of the company's balance sheet.

That, of course, was putting it mildly.

It seemed fitting to have a wake for Dad rather than a funeral. We held it at his local tennis club, a place where Dad had spent so much of his time. It was a party and was well attended for someone who was among the last of his peers to leave this world. It impressed me to see and meet so many people of all different ages who had revered and enjoyed my father for one reason or another.

My brother and I set up a long table with pictures, all of Dad's books, and other memorabilia, including Billy's ceremonial sword, which would always be a big part of our family folklore. Beside the marble box that contained Dad's ashes, we put a bottle of Dewar's Scotch and the rusty old jigger.

Among those who got up to speak was a dear friend of mine who is something of a spiritual channel or medium. She disarmed the room when she told us that Dad's spirit had been hanging around her for a few days. She had never met my father in real life, but said, "My goodness, this is a man with a lot of energy. He doesn't quit, does he? And he wants you all to know he is enjoying the party and loving the attention."

The final person to get up was a beautiful Jamaican woman by the name of Blossom Johnson. Blossom had been one of the dedicated personal-care assistants at the nursing home, and she gave Dad great comfort in his final days. "What about a song, Blossom?" Dad often asked her. And Blossom would oblige.

"Oh when the saints, oh when the saints, oh when the saints go marching in …" she would sing with a fervour that always put a smile on Dad's face.

The very fact that Blossom, a black woman, had made her way into Dad's club, formerly an exclusively white Anglo Saxon establishment, spoke volumes.

"Mr. Bishop was not a religious man," she said before the crowd in her lilting island accent, "but he believed in God. I told him many times that God was with him in the war and that he was with him now. He said his father always told him that, too. And so I say, God bless Arthur Bishop!" she boomed.

"God bless Arthur Bishop," we all repeated.

My friend was right. Dad would have loved it.

* * *

A few months later, as I was sorting through Dad's affairs, I found a letter from Billy to Dad that I hadn't seen before. It was typewritten on flimsy carbon paper. The first page was missing, but I can assume from the content that Billy had written it just after I was born when we were living in Edmonton. It was just a couple of years before Billy died.

> It is difficult for a father to say certain things to a son who he adores and admires. I therefore am writing because I would be much too shy to say to you face to face what I think of you. I only keep on reminding myself that why shouldn't I be proud of you? After all, whose son are you?
>
> It sounds so stupid, but Laddy, I am damn proud of you. I might say that you were very lucky in things such as having me as a father and the world's angel for a mother, thanks of course, by the way and trouble I took in so training her.

And that is one of the awful snags of you being so far away, not that I won't be seeing you, but I won't be seeing the sweet sweet Cydo (my mother) and the Boobit. That latter one I am looking forward to really spoiling.

It was the only record I have of Billy addressing us as a family, and me in particular, showing both a sensitive side and a rather playful one at that, although I could see how it might also be construed as slightly arrogant. But really, to me, it was a gift. The ghost of Billy Bishop was sending me love and telling me he and Dad were together now.

Bill and I buried Dad's ashes next to his father in the Owen Sound cemetery. Yes, it was now me looking down on my father's grave, surrounded by generations of Bishops.

I silently said to myself, *Give 'em the old salute.*

And God bless Arthur Bishop.

CHAPTER 24

COURAGE

I had now lost both my parents and all of my grandparents, and I had no partner or children of my own. I felt lost, alone — even abandoned — and I began to ponder who I was without them.

My life was completely my own now. I was no longer needed as the dutiful daughter, and I wasn't sure how to adjust to that. But I was also very grateful that I had been able to forgive my father before he died because I realized how great a part of my life I'd spent being angry with him and just how much energy that had taken from me.

It also dawned on me that now that our parents' generation was gone, I, along with my brother and our three cousins, had become the purveyors of the Bishop legacy. I regularly handle inquiries about Billy Bishop and his enduring brand. What I especially enjoy is being contacted by a public or high-school student doing a history project on my grandfather. One such letter in particular stands out.

Dear Ms. Bishop,

My name is Ben Allen and I am a Grade 8 student at Ormiston Public School in Whitby, Ontario. Every year, all students in Grade 8 participate in "the Greatest Canadian History Fair." Each student must select one Canadian to be profiled as having made the greatest impact on Canada, Canadians, and on the world.

> Ms. Bishop, I have selected your grandfather, Billy Bishop as my Greatest Canadian!

Ben went on to write the reasons he selected my grandfather. He had been impressed that Billy Bishop "joined the Royal Military College of Canada at such a young age" (just seventeen). He marvelled at Billy's "no-holds-barred style of flying" and thought Billy was "a mastermind in a plane."

Ben kindly invited me to attend the fair at his school. As in other cases, I wrote back thanking him for his letter and giving him some stories and photos that he could use for his exhibit while politely declining his invitation to attend. I was busy, and anyway, I thought that might be a bit much if I showed up; after all, it wasn't about me.

However, Shardie encouraged me to reconsider, sensing it might be cathartic for me to go. "Now that your father is gone, it might be good for you to be reminded of the impact of your heritage up close and personal. And imagine what it would mean to Ben to have a memory like that!"

I decided to rearrange my schedule and surprise Ben.

On the day of the Greatest Canadian History Fair at Ormiston Public School, I drove the thirty minutes to Whitby. I found the auditorium, which was teeming with teachers, kids, parents, and the displays about other famous Canadians like Laura Secord, Pierre Trudeau, and Céline Dion.

I finally spotted young Ben, dressed in a khaki army uniform — the closest thing to a military one he could probably find — and sporting the most adorable fake moustache, which had been the fashion during the world wars. Both my father and grandfather had them.

As I approached, Ben broke into a smile and asked, "Are you Diana?"

"I am," I said, and Ben, at a loss for words, gave me a wide grin. (Ok, I admit I have a need to feel like a celebrity from time to time, even when it isn't really about me. That I get from my father!)

While his mother, Susan, had us pose for pictures, Ben showed me his professional-looking display that included all the pictures I had sent him of Billy. He'd even displayed the letter I had written back to him. I presented Ben with a leather-bound edition of my grandfather's book, *Winged Warfare*, one of the few copies I have of it, and then left on a high.

As the principal of the school walked me out, she commented, "I don't think you realize what a wonderful thing you have done."

I nodded, thinking that she had no idea what Ben had just done for me.

I learned later that Ben got an A on his history project about Billy. I joked that it vindicated the paltry B+ I got for mine when I was his age. (I like to think my teacher was trying to make sure that I did not get a swelled head writing about my own grandfather. I know I deserved an A!) Ben graduated grade eight with high marks and was the school's valedictorian that year. He promised me that one of these days he would hold a dinner party where everything would be served backwards, just as Billy had done way back when. I told him he had better invite me!

It heartens me to hear from other young people of Ben's generation, who are now even farther removed from the direct experiences of family members who experienced the world wars. They are interested in the history, and some are connecting with personal stories about the individuals themselves by selecting someone, a soldier who died at the Somme, or a pilot who flew in the Battle of Britain, for example, and then researching where they came from, who their family was, and where they found the courage to go to war.

I also continue to meet people who want to know more about my grandfather. Interestingly, most of them have never heard about the controversy surrounding his credentials, or if they have, they say it doesn't really matter to them. I believe that history will treat my grandfather well in that respect. My brother put it best in a foreword he wrote for a reprint of *Winged Warfare*: "A thousand years from now when humanity is crossing the galaxy in starships, their pilots and passengers will look back at the exploits of Billy Bishop and the other pilots of the Great War, and say, 'That's how it all began ...'"

That is the legacy that will survive the test of time and it makes me burst with renewed pride.

* * *

It took a while, but I allowed myself to fully grieve the loss of my parents. I didn't stuff it down or try to cover it up. I had learned that it was better to feel the depths of one's sorrow than to bottle it up like they did, and so I allowed myself to fully mourn the loss of a part of my life in which my grandparents and parents played principal roles. It was awkward at first to think that I could be the star of my own life, but now that I have embraced that idea, I feel grounded, calmer, and more myself with each and every day. That's because I recognize, finally, that I have been given and have also taken the very best of my family. My brother and I have both consciously nurtured the choice bits of our mother, father, grandmother, and grandfather within ourselves. I certainly have Billy's sense of adventure, enthusiasm, and inclination to think big. And I inherited my father's sense of humour, creativity, and most importantly, his love of a story. And Dad had so much to teach me, even from his faults.

Growing up in a chaotic environment where you are always looking to maintain control can be a gift if you choose to look at it that way. I became highly sensitive, developing an extra ability to feel, adapt to, and even foreshadow the moods and needs of others. I have always been someone who can walk into a room and immediately gravitate to the one person who feels awkward or isolated. I have an acute sense of empathy, and am able to put myself in the place of another to experience what they are feeling and understand their motives and desires. Once upon a time this aptitude made me sick. I felt things too deeply. I took on others' emotional pain. But I have turned this potential negative into a positive, relying on it to guide me purposefully in my life.

When I was a reporter, it helped me to interview people with compassion and responsiveness. I could bring an emotional element to the story that made people care and, I hoped, take some action if required, such as reaching out to someone in need or galvanizing public support for an issue or cause.

That ability also formed the centrepiece of my business, which has proven to be the greatest gift of my professional life. I work with the kinds of extraordinary people whom I met growing up and that I interviewed and admired as a journalist — from politicians, scientists, and doctors to entrepreneurs and Fortune 500 executives, as well as ballet dancers, fashion designers, and beauty pageant contestants. It all fits, doesn't it? That someone whose family had such a public image to uphold and protect would end up in an image and branding business.

It is with enormous gratitude that I can say it has evolved into so much more. I seem to attract clients who are on an inspired mission of one kind or another and who want to clarify and focus their stories. It often requires finding and releasing the emotional blocks that stand in their way. That seems to be my true calling: helping people to reframe their life stories to reveal who they really are and the unique value they provide — something that took me a long time to do for myself.

Yes, I am proud to be the granddaughter of one of the greatest, bravest, most daring fighter pilots who ever lived — a man who explored the boundaries of human courage by setting an example for others to follow. Along this journey, I have discovered that I need heroes in my life to inspire and motivate me to try new things, to make every bit of my life matter, and to be the best version of myself. I have come to appreciate the fact that sometimes the most unlikely people can turn out unexpectedly to be your hero, as happened with my father. As it turned out, he taught me the greatest lesson I had to learn: forgiveness.

And finally, I have learned that the face of a hero has changed, not just for me, but for all of us. Of course, we continue to celebrate those who achieve the big breakthroughs, such as Canada's first female astronaut Roberta Bondar. But the modern face of heroism is now more likely to be someone who saves or protects lives rather than taking them, like the two U.S. servicemen and the civilian who took down an armed jihadist aboard a French train, or Corporal Nathan Cirillo, who was gunned down while standing guard at the National War Memorial in Ottawa in 2014. Our heroes are more human now. And we see our former heroes a little differently — no longer in just black and white but with added touches of grey. They are not perfect. And that's okay.

As for my father, he might have had a much easier life if he had decided to take a different course than his father. But he didn't. He took the same path. And while valiantly serving his country, he was devotedly upholding and honouring the legacy of his famous father. Dad was also able to leave his own legacy, a substantial one, by honouring the stories of our country's war heroes that future generations will continue to read. Living in the shadow of his father was difficult; it brought out both the best and worst in him. Dad wasn't able to slay all of his demons, but he found the courage to survive and excel.

I think about how things might have been different if people had talked about PTSD in my grandparents' and parents' days the way they do today. Perhaps my father would have received the help he needed. Instead, in their respective postwar eras, they told each other their amusing stories while they self-medicated with copious cocktails. The silent trauma they had all experienced was swept under the collective carpet. The result was unresolved hurt, suppressed suffering, and neuroses that followed them into their home lives and were passed on to their families to deal with.

It was our family secret. And I know that many families like mine with parents and grandparents who served in the First and Second World Wars had the same secret. I speculate that it is still a symptom of war, and more of us should be sharing our stories and how we are dealing with them.

On the lighter side of things, I wonder, if my father had known that I would write a memoir in which he would have a starring role, would he have behaved better? I chuckle because I honestly doubt it — he might have treated my mother better, but overall Dad enjoyed being outrageous and loved his notoriety. My friend, the spiritual channeller, assures me that Dad is up there looking down, waving at all of us and loving the attention.

I hope both my parents are smiling down on me, appreciating from their hallowed perspective that in some strange and wonderful way I survived them. I survived this family. And I have put things right for myself. Where Dad could never expose his vulnerability in having a legend to live up to, and my mother could not break free from emotional exile, I gave myself the gift of self-exploration that helped me realize I could be myself and love and appreciate this person. It has allowed me to follow my own path, to be a woman who is not defined by social expectations, and to find her own power in that. It has allowed me to fulfill myself in a wonderful career that uses so many of the skills my parents taught me and has brought me a sense of purpose and great joy. It has allowed me to be and feel successful in my own right, finally. Yes, it may have taken me a long time to get here, and perhaps this is true for many of us, but I truly cherish this new sense of self. And most importantly, it has allowed me to finally feel like I am enough.

I am good enough.

So while I have never gone to war, engaged in aerial combat (or even flown a plane!), I have summoned every bit of courage that I have to write this story and to expose myself and my family in this way. There were members of my family who asked me why I did it, and I told them it was just something I knew I had to do. It was like a gift I was giving to myself — because it allowed me to let go of emotional baggage that didn't really belong to me. When I liberated myself from my family history and my sense of what was expected of me, I found it made me appreciate my family even more.

I believe that each generation builds on the experiences of the last, so in telling my story, I've sought not only to mend and heal my own pain, but perhaps a little of my parents' and grandparents', too. This is where I found my own courage. And discovered that there is a hero in all of us.

IMAGE CREDITS

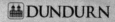